Enjoy!
L x

YOUR
SALON RETAIL

The no-nonsense, no-hype guide to kick-arse retail in your salon business.

LISA CONWAY

Published by Zing Office in 2017.

© Lisa Conway 2017

National Library of Australia Cataloguing-in-Publication entry
Creator: Conway, Lisa, author.

Title: Your salon retail: The no nonsense, no hype guide to kick-arse retail in your salon business / Lisa Conway.

ISBN: 978-0-6480162-0-5 (pbk.)

Subjects: Beauty shops--Australia--Management.
Hairdressing--Australia--Management
Success in business--Australia.

Dewey Number: 646.72420681

Disclaimer
The material in this publication is of the nature of general comment only, and does not represent professional advice. It is not intended to provide specific guidance for particular circumstances and it should not be relied on as the basis for any decision to take action or not take action on any matter which it covers. Readers should obtain professional advice where appropriate, before making any such decision. The author and publisher disclaim all responsibility and liability to any person, arising directly or indirectly from any person taking or not taking action based on the informaton in this publication.

Front Cover photography: Jason Malouin www.portraitstore.com.au
Back Cover photography: Jason Malouin www.portraitstore.com.au
Editing: www.overthepage.com.au
Front Cover design: www.thesqueezebox.com.au
Internal page layout: www.thesqueezebox.com.au
Illustrations: www.holopress.net
Printing: Minuteman Press Prahran www.minutemanpressprahran.com.au 60221

This book is dedicated to Jay and Marie,
who strapped in for the ride …
long before we knew what an amazing ride
ZING was going to be.

The THANK YOU page.

There are people in your life and then there are people in your life. I am blessed with the best of the best. I'd like to personally thank the A team that we call ZING.

Andrea Kallinikos, who before joining ZING was and still is my best friend. Thank you for never trying to slow me down or box me in. Thank you for every T you cross and every I you dot. For doing whatever I ask, and for just trusting there is a method to my madness. For accepting that the goal posts move and believing in me and the process that we call ZING. One of the many reasons I love you to bits.

Simon McCulloch, not only are you my lover, you are my best friend. You inspire me to bigger and better things every day. Together we have six kids and a dog, and we are blessed to want for nothing. We have it all. Thank you for steering me around the potholes and preventing me from bumping into walls. You challenge me to think and act on a grander scale and I love you to the moon and back.

David Dugan, my coach. You saw in me what I couldn't see or dare to believe was possible. You took my business, Zingers and all, from the pushbike lane we were riding in to the formula one track we are now on today. Thank you for challenging me to play a bigger game and calling me on my bullshit that was holding me back. Big squeeze.

Andrew Griffith, who absolutely is the biggest spunk of all. You taught me the art of storytelling and encouraged me to find my voice. You saw a writer within and you simply added water and sunshine to a hidden talent I didn't know I had. Big kiss … *mwah!* times ten.

Sheryl Allen, my golden retriever, loyal, gentle and kind. Through your nurturing, you managed to turn my dog's breakfast of a manuscript into the polished version I can share here today. Life is better because of you and I can't thank you enough. Love your work and I love you, too.

Jay Chapman, for offering what "I need" long before I even think to ask. For adding to whatever idea I come up with and making it even better. You are my madness buddy and your company is delightful. You are always thinking about how we can play a bigger game and that inspires me. Big hug.

Marie Drever, who takes being organised to a whole new level. Your ability to gently point out that it could be even better if we just added this idea to the plan. Your talent and generosity is endless. You are so much more than lipstick and pearls. You are always adding value to the cake mixture we call ZING. Big hug.

CONTENTS

CONTENTS

"Surround yourself only with people who are going to take you higher."

Oprah Winfrey

FOREWORD

There are people we meet who are happy to follow the status quo and then there are people we meet who are destined to challenge the world as we know it.

Lisa Conway is most certainly one of the latter.

I've had the enormous pleasure of getting to know Lisa over the past 3 years, helping her to write her first book *The Naked Salon*. Since then she has gone on to write a wonderful second book *Your Salon Team* and of course, you're holding her third book *Your Salon Retail* in your hot little hands. I love them all, I'm impressed by them all and I get the feeling this is just the beginning.

Lisa is one of those people who knows her industry incredibly well. She thrives on everything about it and her passion is to help others to be as successful as they can be. Lisa will do everything she can to help them achieve this. This shines through in her no-nonsense approach to writing and coaching her salon clients that is getting extraordinary results around Australia.

Watching Lisa in front of a crowd – sharing her own story, her own trials and tribulations as well as her own successes – and it's impossible not to love and adore her. Her brutal honesty comes with a cheeky grin, but the home truths Lisa delivers are exactly what this industry needs. In fact, many industries need to hear what she has to say.

I have no doubt that you will get a great deal out of Your Salon Retail, but I'm going to say this is just one part of the extraordinary solution that Lisa offers. Read all of her books, go to her events, work with her – and your business will never be the same again. And I promise it will be a blast every step of the way.

Andrew Griffiths,
International Bestselling Business Author,
Speaker and Mentor.

PREFACE

Every time I hear the Chicken Dance* tune, I smile.

If you have no idea what I mean by the Chicken Dance, Google it now.

The Chicken Dance carries me back to my early years of hairdressing. Thirty years on, it still stops me in my tracks. Here's why.

It was the early eighties. I was 21 and had just moved to Melbourne. One of the girls I worked with invited me to her wedding along with 500 or so other guests. Yes, it was an Italian wedding, my very first one.

The weddings I'd been to before were held in the town hall of my rural hometown (population 900, provided no one was away on holiday). The catering was always cold meat and salad topped off with trifle provided by the town's church ladies.

So, on this night, at a big Italian wedding in the city, my eyes stuck out on stalks like you'd see on a prawn at the Queen Victoria Market. There was a lot to take in.

Never in my life had I seen so many short, plump women dressed to the nines. Talk about mutton done up as lamb. The room was full of them! A few looked like they'd been buttered and rolled in a box of sequins. The effort they went to was fabulous.

The men were also well-dressed in suits and they spent time dancing with the hundred or so children. The young ladies looked like meringues in their little puffy dresses.

There was enough food to feed my hometown for a week!

It was absolutely mental and I loved every minute of it.

Just when I thought it couldn't get any better, the Chicken Dance came on. The Nonnas and Nonnos all jumped up on the dance floor. Everyone knew the moves. A warm feeling came over me and I was so glad I'd taken the plunge and moved to Melbourne. The farmers in my town were not the Chicken Dance type. They were far too conservative.

I knew I was in the right place at the right time with the right people. Although I didn't get most of what was going, I felt like I fitted in.

There and then, I fell in love with the madness of it all. It became my happy thought. Whenever I was working away on the salon floor, making suggestions on either retail or service, and nailed the client connection – enough to get a *That's fabulous advice, I will take all three products, thank you.* or *Any chance we can do that today? I'm so excited.* – that tune played in my head.

It still does.

It's always been the icing on my happy cake. YES, it's madness, but I wouldn't change it for anything.

That Chicken Dance reminds me of why I'm where I am today.

Our industry is connected by emotion. It's a people-to-people world. At any time, with no warning, a huge wave of "happy" can sneak up on you. It's when I say to myself, "F#^*k I love what I do!" I know I'm in the right place at the right time, with the right people and right in the middle of me thinking "I'm so happy" things go up a notch and I hear:

Da da da da da da dah, da da da da da da dah, da da da da. Da da da da da da dah, da da da da da da dah da da da da. Quack Quack Quack.

Da da da da da da dah, da da da da da da dah, da da da da. Da da da da da da dah, da da da da da da dah da da da da. Quack Quack Quack.

La la lah and so on.

If you're not in this industry, you won't get what I'm saying. It's nailing a blow wave that you know will stop traffic. It's rinsing a colour that's even better than you thought. It's getting paid to laugh. It's a client sending you thank you flowers. It's the cha-ching of the cash register at the end of a big day. It's client's grateful hug that's so tight you fear your head might pop off. Or the phone call from a client to say the baby's arrived, no stitches!

It's in that magical moment, right there, that I hear that stupid song in my head.

It's my I'm-in-the-right-place-at-the-right-time-with-the-right-people song.

We go out of our way to please. We're wired in a way that we can't help but come in early for clients, stay back late for clients, round down the price and squeeze in our favourites, all because we're chasing that sweet spot when BOOM! – that stupid Chicken Dance (da da da da da da dah, da da da da da da dah, da da da da) comes to mind.

It's that moment when you think: *This is why I do what I do!*

Da da da da da da dah, da da da da da da dah, da da da da. Da da da da da da dah, da da da da da da dah da da da da. Quack Quack Quack.

Da da da da da da dah, da da da da da da dah, da da da da. Da da da da da da dah, da da da da da da dah da da da da.

Caring for the right client at the right time for the right reason feels this good.

Every single time.

Quack Quack Quack.

one

chapter

1

Retail is not a dirty word.

If anyone ever learnt retail the hard way, it was me. Let me tell you about the disastrous void-of-business smarts headspace I came from. It could only ever be up from there. I take no pride in how small-minded I was. But with that behind me, and countless first-hand lessons under my belt, I've now trained hundreds and hundreds of retail sceptics just like you.

Hopefully you're here reading this book because you're having second thoughts. Maybe you've heard you're missing out. I'm here to tell you: if you're ignoring the potential of retail in your salon you're missing out BIGTIME. And on so many levels. Read on and learn salon retail smarts – the why, the how, the who, the when, the what, the tips, the tricks, the what-to-do and the what-not-to-do. You'll thank me when your retail sales kick arse.

1

Change in itself is not difficult.

Lasting change is a whole other beast – you must open your head to learning and your heart to pleasing.

A retail business humming along inside your salon business is the difference between camping under the stars and staying in a 5-star hotel. The choice is yours. Money gives you choices and retail will give you the money.

Read on. I'll tell you what to do and when to do it. More importantly, I'll tell you why to do it. Know that I have your best interests at heart. That means giving you the good oil about retail without the fluff or bullshit spin. Nothing but the real deal. Let's do this!

Once a hairdresser, always a hairdresser.

I'm a hairdresser through and through. Although I no longer work on the floor cutting hair, I still consider myself a hairdresser. I didn't do an apprenticeship; I did a 12-month full-time course. At the end, when I expected to be snapped up, I struggled to get a job. The year was 1984 and there was a glut of hairdressers. Back then, if you kicked a bush (any bush) out jumped a hairdresser. That's a very country Australian thing to say. I'm not apologising. I am exactly that, an Aussie.

Yes, I did manage to secure my first job. And later found out my hiring was based on my look. We're such a visual crowd. I deliberately played that card and showed up looking my absolute best. I stayed with that company, the one that hired me based on my look, for the next 16 years. And, for the most part I loved it.

I had a fabulous boss but I yearned to do my own thing, have my own version of a salon. I decided it was time to move on. You know how it is: you wake up one day and you've already decided you can do what your boss does (even better) out on your own. My business plan was basic at best. All I wanted to do was work closer to my three children who were all in primary school. My mind was made up. I was leaving.

My husband, a secondary school maths teacher, figured I'd be OK if my takings topped $1300 a week, adding that $2000 would be unreal. My first week's takings were $3000 … and I never looked back.

" A retail business humming along inside your salon business is the *difference between camping under the stars and staying in a 5-star hotel.* **"**

Three years in, I was making my original target of $1300 each week in retail sales alone. Talk about the icing on a fabulous cake, right there! It wasn't always like that; it certainly had its crappy moments, huge challenges and many, many tears. But I wouldn't swap a single day because everything I learned back then has made me the version of me I am today. I love that as

1

a salon coach there is nothing a salon owner faces that hasn't happened to me. I've walked a mile in your shoes. It gives me the empathy I need to be an awesome coach.

There are no mistakes in life, there are only lessons.

I'm going to share with you the lessons I learnt about recommending retail to your salon clients.

When I left my boss Sam, it was on good terms. I moved far enough away that I was never a threat to his business. That's the best you can hope for when you lose a team member with a big clientele.

Sam always said if I did the right thing by him (not open up across the road) he'd help me get established. And he did. We had many chats around how I might price my services and grow my business. I was starting from absolutely nothing. I think back now and know I was naïve. Maybe I wouldn't be so brave today. But being ignorant likely worked in my favour.

I can remember Sam asking me what I planned to do about retail. My response? *Nah, I can't be bothered.* Sam strongly suggested I make some sort of an effort. Thinking back, I had no idea, did I? Naïve AND lazy – it's a miracle I ever got this far.

I just wanted to look after my clients and not bother with retail. *I'm not in sales, I'm a hairdresser.* I now know that sentence makes no sense at all. It came from a place of ignorance. It wasn't until years down the track that I encountered Michelle, one of the most engaging product company representatives ever. She started me from ground zero and taught me the power of retail. It's a superpower and I'm going to share it with you along with everything I've learnt over thirty-plus years in our industry.

I'm going to be totally upfront. I invite you to have a laugh at my expense and then get on with the job of recommending retail to your loyal customers and to the ones you've not even met yet. Why? Because everyone deserves your expert recommendations when it comes to looking after their hair and skin, and all their beauty needs between visits. Together, you and each client are working on the best possible outcome. That has to be a good thing.

Back to my story.

I opened the door of my new salon with a staff of one. Yes, just little old me. The couple of boxes of products Sam gave me were not the ones I favoured, so they sat there and gathered dust – one of the reasons I didn't want retail in the first place. I hate dusting. I never do it. *We have people for that* (in a toffy high-pitched voice). FYI: I've had a housekeeper ever since I was pregnant with my twins. My gynaecologist recommended it and I was all over that win like a fat kid to a cupcake. The very same day, I found a housekeeper and have never looked back. Twenty-five years on and I still don't dust.

Yet, here I was: a new salon owner with a shelf of dusty products that I wouldn't recommend to anyone. Here's the thing – hair and beauty professionals are genuine people. If we don't like it, we sure as hell aren't going to recommend it. We're wired that way. We only share what we love. Our opinion matters more

than anything. That's where your success lies. You must work on changing your opinion on the products you stock or you're wasting your time.

There was one product I absolutely loved working with. It was called FAT Hair. Don't ask me who made it. I remember a client showing me how well it worked. Like a true hairdresser, I told everyone about it. We're exceptional at spreading good news. And FAT Hair was great news: it made otherwise limp, fine and flyaway hair "fatten up" and stay put.

Naturally, I told my clients that when they were in town, they should pop into a particular store and pick-up this amazing product. The store was about 50km away but everyone went to town for something, so I didn't see it as an inconvenience. I cringe now at my sheer ignorance.

One day a client said to me, "Why don't you get ten or so and put them here on the shelf. Even if you added a couple of bucks on for your trouble, you'd be saving us the trouble of getting it for ourselves."

Gotta love clients with great ideas! She was absolutely right. Not because two dollars a product was much benefit to me but because I was helping my clients to get the product they needed.

When I was next in town, I wandered through the big hair product warehouse looking for FAT Hair. They must have moved it. When I asked the sales assistant about it, she replied, "What the hell! Another one?"

She then explained that I was the third person that day looking for FAT Hair. She asked, "Are you from Gisborne, too?" The look on my face as I answered *YES* must have been priceless.

"It must be good," she said. "They all want it."

Drawing of Products on a shelf one labelled FAT hair

That day I decided to rethink my approach to retail. I realised people were taking my advice on board and wanted to use the products I recommended. I needed to have everything my client needed on hand in the salon so they could be looking after themselves in between visits to me. In other words, that day I decided to grow up and be a proper salon owner with retail and all. I pulled on my big girl pants.

" *People buy from people they know, like and trust.* "

About a week later a bloke came into my salon just on closing time. He was well-dressed and had a lovely smiley face. That matters to me. His name was Rob and he was state manager for a big organisation owned by Proctor and Gamble, the biggest of the biggest. His company PPS (Professional Products for Salons) was doing well at the time. He said he lived just up the street, and although he travelled across Australia he would be more than happy to drop off some products for me to see if

I liked them. He said his wife was a hairdresser and the word about town was I was rocking it.

Rob said, "You will only sell them if you like them so let's just see if you like them first. If you do, we can talk then."

He dropped off 8 to 10 products the following week. We tried them (there were two of us by then) and we loved them. My junior was so excited that the products were brightly coloured, making it easy for her to learn which was which. The rest is history.

We worked through all the issues we all face when it comes to direct selling. The difference was we persevered until we overcame them. We became one of Rob's best salons, that is, the ones with the highest monthly spend. It took us about two years. By then I had a team of five and we introduced another company's brand into the mix. We had a complete system that worked and we stuck to it. There was plenty of trial, heaps of error but we kept on keeping on and made it work.

It's all about you.

Like anything new to you, to make it work you must want to change. I'm here to open the door on your thinking. As is true for everything in life, the problem is you. It's always you and that's the good news, because if you want to change you don't have to ask for anyone's permission. You alone are the solution.

Read on and let me challenge your limiting beliefs, the ones that stop you from sticking to the system that you so loosely put in place. I'll show you how to hush that negative voice that

1

tells you your clients already have everything or don't have the money. Those and every other bullshit excuse under the sun. I'm going to show you how to kick every excuse to the kerb.

I know for sure there is a powerful link between customer loyalty and retail sales. That's the most exciting part. Remember my clients driving 50km to do what I suggested? If that isn't loyalty, nothing is.

People buy from people they know, like and trust. You don't have to actively "sell" to move retail, you just have to focus on the loyalty and tell your clients the truth.

If I can do it, you can do it. Now, let's get started. Let's kick some arse.

Kick-arse kick-starter.

Take a 5-minute survey of your shelf of dusty products. How many (if any) do you love? How many could you genuinely recommend to a favourite client?

two

chapter

Show and tell – in that order

Your *I'm not in sales* mindset is the first thing we need to change. I'm coming across that statement less often than I used to – a good sign that we're making progress.

As I said before, *I'm not in sales* is a bullshit statement. You're probably using it because you're hiding from reality or don't understand how sales work. It's your excuse for not doing your job, for justifying a "near enough" way of servicing clients. It's 100% about you, not your clients. We're in the service industry. We service people. Holding back information from them is NOT servicing.

I'm not in sales is your opinion. It's how you see the world … or at least how you've seen things up until now. You're reading this book so you know there must be a better way. Here it is.

The dictionary meaning of "sales" is: *The exchange of a commodity for money; the action of selling something.*

2

The second part of that definition relates to our industry's way of thinking. *The action of selling something* expresses my thinking that you can sell an idea. Believing that sales is only related to money falls short. You sell the idea and *that* relates to the money. It's like a person who sells cars. That makes him a car salesman. Sure, you pay money for the car but first the salesperson has to convince you that it's the right car choice for you, that you're going to look and feel good in this car, and that it fits your budget. Then and only then will you hand over your hard-earned in exchange for the car.

In that sense he's a salesperson. If you explain to your client the benefits to her of the skin care or hair care you want her to start using, then and only then will she take your advice and purchase the product.

So, it's the same. Yet, unlike the car industry where they boast about the salesperson being good at sales, we don't. Why not? Why don't we showcase and reward the best in the industry? Why don't we say, "Meet Sarah, a great stylist with amazing retail sales. She is a retail machine. She just won retail salesperson for the state of Victoria."

Hands up those who would want to employ Sarah. I thought so. Form an orderly queue, people.

Why not celebrate retail success?

What if product companies showcased not only the best salons in terms of retail sales, but also the best individual salespeople within the salon? First prize could be a car, or lunch with

George Clooney. OK, now I'm getting overexcited. But let's stop and think for a minute. Imagine if the big companies had a competition maybe over a year to showcase the best salespeople. The top 100 might be invited to a National Gala Dinner at the best restaurant in town, perhaps with a celebrity thrown in for a real wow! The top 10 might each get a MacBook Pro (or similar), and the winner an all-expenses paid trip to Paris for a week. We can work the details out later. We just need to inject some *OMG!* into it, make it something for everyone to aspire to. Imagine if celebrating retail sales was one of the things that drew salons to a product company. I think it would definitely work the other way, drawing product companies to the winning salons.

" *Why not?* *Why don't we* showcase *and* reward the best in the industry? "

Product companies would need to get serious about education in retail sales. Most of them would have to triple the effort they put in now. They'd have to run boot camps for all team members and be across the entire mindset of retail. That could only be a good thing.

Everyone's a winner.

Everyone wins when a client leaves with a product.

The salon stylist, therapist connects on a trust level and upgrades a client to an A or B.

The product company makes money from the sale.

The product rep makes budget and bonus. That feels great.

And the biggest win of all is **the client** having her problem solved.

All the while **the salon owner** is building a better brand and being paid for it.

The only down is you must keep up with the demands of ordering and maybe dusting the stock. Here's a plan: sell them so fast they don't get a chance to collect dust.

There are a couple of brands doing retail training well. Notice I said "a couple". I believe it's something EVERY brand should aim for.

What are you really selling?

2

Let's go back to the word "selling" and get really clear on it. To me selling someone something is a way of getting them to understand your idea or your point of view. In the case of the car salesman, that you'd look hot in this car, it will be a reliable means of transport or it will easily fit the golf clubs or the pram in the back. In simple terms, selling is getting your point across to the interested party. When the other person buys your story or shares your vision, they agree they'd be better off with whatever you're selling them. They understand the benefits to them.

For example, if I want to go to the 9 o'clock movie instead of the 7 o'clock session, I'll explain to my girlfriend that sitting in a cinema while you're starving makes it difficult to concentrate. When we come out of the 9 o'clock movie most restaurants will have already closed their kitchens. I'll suggest we eat first at seven and then go into the later session. I'm selling this to my girlfriend (quite well, I might add). I'm pointing out the benefits of my idea, but not asking her for any money. It's still a sale. I've sold her on the idea.

Selling is as much about ideas as it is about products.

I travel often and when I'm away I love doing salon research. I find a salon I like the look of and spoil myself by going in and having a blow wave. Yet, I'm very rarely impressed with the stylist's effort to make retail recommendations to me or to even tell me what product they put in my hair.

2 Just the other day I came across a little salon that was as cute as a button. The two people working there were delightful – they even had a salon dog and you can imagine how happy that made me! I was offered champagne, even though it was only 11am. The water was sparkling and so was everything else. It was an all-round fabulous experience. The salon was very cool and spotlessly clean.

I explained I had two meetings that day and was struggling with the local humidity. He said, "Yep, that's cool. I've got some serum that will stop that (easy peasy)." I commented on the products displayed in the window, explaining how I loved one of the conditioners because its copper tint kept my red hair fresh and pumped up.

He continued doing my hair. The minute he started, I knew he was capable so I relaxed and played on Facebook, not concerned at all that I would be unhappy.

But at no point did he share the knowledge he had around the products he used on my hair. Nothing, not a thing. He missed an opportunity to help me out. I wanted that conditioner because I was out of it. On principle, I refused to ask for it and he didn't make a sale. And it would have been helpful for me to take the serum product home with me. It did control the frizz somewhat, so I'd have taken it *and* the conditioner. The real question here is: why didn't he at least share what he knew about the serum?

The answer is this: we have not been trained to recommend products to clients. It's always been a side thing. Some of you even have separate targets for retail. Please stop that. It sends an unconscious message that retail is a separate thing to service. It is not separate … it *is* service.

2

I know what you're thinking. You've trained your staff and they still don't get it. I'm not suggesting you haven't trained them. I'm saying this: to train them right you need to start at the centre. Deal with one team member at a time, unblock what holds them back and get to their reason why. As an industry, we've just started to scratch the surface. We need to get it into our DNA. The way we do this is by showing and telling.

Years back I went to a presentation on customer service. The presenter wasn't from our industry; she was from one of the big banks. Her role was customer complaints (a big gig). She explained they tracked complaints into categories and the most common category was "not being informed/lack of information" meaning the customer didn't know something.

They didn't know they couldn't transfer money out of that account. They didn't know there was a better product available. They didn't know the interest rate was X. The list went on.

We are no different. Our customers mostly have the same category of complaints. They didn't know the treatment at the basin was an extra cost. They didn't know they'd be red like a beetroot for two days after their facial treatment. They didn't know the spray tan would be dark around their ankles and knees due to their dry skin. If they'd known all of these things first, they'd have had a different result. Or they might have prepared differently. If they knew their colour was going to take four hours they might have organised to bring some work with them on their laptop.

2

Not telling, not showing and not informing your customers on every level influences their salon experience big time. It causes misunderstandings and leads to complaints.

Everything can be fixed with a product or a service; they need both. Start showing and telling tomorrow. Never forget: your customer is seeking an experience. They expect you to be an expert in not just what you do but also in the products you use. Telling is not selling – it's sharing your expertise.

Every client, every time.

From this day forward, every time you put your hand on a product and you're about to put it on someone's skin or someone's hair, simply tell them what you're doing and why. Make all your best recommendations your secrets.

Now, let me share one of my secrets with you. I used to hate the way men put hair product on both sides and the top and almost always missed the back. So I'd show them how to apply it properly and describe it like this: "Imagine your product is bright red paint. To get it even you need to tap it everywhere first. You must always tap it first at the back of your head. Why? Because you miss here and it looks bad to everyone else but you. Your hair is always thicker at the back. Tap, tap, tap … like this. When you feel the product's been pulled off your hands, like this, then you can do the rub. It needs to be a gentle rub. No need for a rough rub. Save that for your dog; they love the rough rub. Now, see how you have the back covered and you haven't used nearly as much as you have been at home (mirror to show back)."

If I said that once, I said it thousands of times and I always got a "That's much better, Lisa. Gee, thanks!" My response was always the same: "You're welcome. I'm happy when you're happy."

Somewhere in the sharing of knowledge you'll not only showcase yourself to be the expert you are, you'll wow your clients and foster their trust in you as a professional. Trust me, they'll be grateful for your knowledge. And they'll be much more likely to buy the products you recommend.

Showing your clients what you're doing and telling them why you're doing it … it's kick-arse in natural flow.

Kick-arse kick-starter.

When you're applying product to your own hair (or skin, or nails) today, think about why and how you're doing it. Voice your thoughts out loud to yourself as you go, explaining the secrets you use. There you have it: a genuine "show and tell" script for a favourite product.

three

chapter

3

What doesn't work.

3

Read on. I'll save you learning the hard way. This chunky chapter on "what NOT to do" will save you a truckload of time and effort. When you understand what won't get your salon retail rocking, you can re-focus your energy with laser precision on what will.

Quick fixes.

I've tried all the retail quick fixes in one shape or another. Quick fixes give you a quick fix. Go figure! They're short-lived, hence the name. Take money rewards as an example. The $2 per product sale or any other short-term retail type targets – they don't work. I know because I trialled those too. How about yelling (I tried that too) or any other type of "losing your shit"? They're all just temporary stabs at the real problems. You'll get a little "up" but it wont last. Only changing the way you think about retail can possibly give you the long-term results you want. That's what this book is all about.

Listening to your own BS excuses.

The answer lies in learning more about yourself and your history up until today. You need to be honest about why you haven't had any real success in shifting retail. Call your excuses for the BS they are (refer to Chapter 5). It's different for everyone. For most of you, it's a combination of things. The solution is all about being truthful with yourself and getting on with making the little shifts. Eventually, you'll get to a place where the effort is no longer conscious. Recommending retail to clients will simply be what you do. It's so normal, you don't even know you're doing it.

> **First, be honest about your shortcomings. Second, get the training you need to nail retail once and for all.**

Making giant leaps.

There's a speech in the movie *Any Given Sunday* that's worth the YouTube search. I listen to it when I need a reminder that it's the small steps, the micro-decisions you make every day that get you the results. In the movie, the team is down and Al Pacino addresses them by saying:

"We need to fight our way back one inch at a time. Life is a game of inches. When you add up all those inches. That is what is going to make the fucking difference between winning and losing."

It gives me goose bumps *every* time. You can apply this theory to any situation where you feel trapped, lost or overwhelmed by the task. Make a start and celebrate every inch or, in your case, every product sale.

Relying on quick fixes (yes, I'll say it again).

Think of quick fixes in your retail like fad diets with your weight. First we need to address the word "diet". That word doesn't mean weight loss; diet simply means what you consume. It's the same with "sales". It doesn't mean only the transfer of money; it's the ability to sell an idea.

"Diet" is so heavily connected to weight loss that we go straight to weight loss when we hear the word diet. The same could be said for retail sales.

Fad diets are nothing more than a desperate approach to a long-standing and bigger underlying problem. When it comes to your salon retail, "sales" is the same. Neither works long-term. At best, either might give you a quick, short-term result. The only way to lose weight long-term is eat a LOT LESS and move a LOT MORE. Yes, it's that simple. We get all tangled up about it but the truth is we're putting way more fuel in our tanks than we need to make the energy we burn. We don't need that much fuel so we store it and get heavier and heavier. Most of us are eating enough fuel to keep a 21-year-old Olympic athlete powered. The trouble is we're moving like a 90-year-old in a retirement village!

There's no shortage of education about healthy eating, so why do we keep gaining weight? And product companies claim to be educating us about retail sales so why, as an industry, are we so useless at it?

Thinking retail is a one-trick dog.

You make choices every day. You need to focus on choosing to learn the things that hold you back. Concentrate on your WHY. *Why am I still not there with my retail? Why do I have some good weeks and some bad weeks? Why does it all turn pear-shaped the minute I stop reminding them to do their job?*

It's not one thing; the reasons are many and I outline them all in this book. Read it from start to finish. Every chapter. Every page. If you're jumping from chapter to chapter, you're seeking a quick fix … you fad dieter, you! I wrote it in this order for a reason. Do things the right way and take the time to fix it once.

This book is not the lemon detox version; it's about going back to what you want for your customer. If it's what I hope it is – to be the best hairdresser, beauty therapist or skin specialist there is for them – you must do more than just read my book. You must go down my Truth and Training path.

First, be honest about your shortcomings. Second, get the training you need to nail retail once and for all. Your clients will love you for it. I promise.

Recommending retail is a skill you have to learn, practise and perfect. Quick fixes simply aren't sustainable. If you want lasting change you need to get back to basics and forget the short-term targets (at least for now). So, why do product companies insist on short-term challenges and a reward system for great selling? Because, just like the "Shit, the wedding is next week, I need to do a detox diet" panic, there are short-term gains to be had. Is it going to fix your problem long-term? Absolutely not. It's just a boost along. Some of your team might respond well to using bonuses and targets. Others won't enjoy the focus or the pressure. These learnings are helpful – they get you a step closer to whatever holds them back from consistently performing.

There's nothing wrong with friendly competition. You might even surprise yourself with how your focus shifts. Just remember: it's only ever short-term. You need to stop dangling a carrot in front of someone to tempt them to do their job. Instead, educate them as to why doing their job properly is the right thing to do and in the best interests of everyone, most importantly the client. Never forget the 5-Point Star, and who is the star. It requires all five of you to work as a team.

You're the only one who can make the star work. Every success or failure depends on you and your relationship with the client. Recommending products and services to your clients is your job. I'm going to say it again because nothing is more important: recommending products and services to your clients is your job. Period.

Forgetting why you started.

Remind yourself and your team why you joined the industry in the first place. Hopefully it was to make someone look and feel beautiful and that requires problem-solving 101. The client comes in with a problem and we solve it. The way to solve a problem for someone is to first find out what the problem is. Then you simply solve that problem with either a product or service. If you train your team from a position of honesty and integrity, it will stick with them forever.

Imagine not having to say, "Don't forget to recommend today". It's possible when you choose to learn this new skill.

Letting the appointment book boss you around.

You must change your thinking from doing the service task, to also doing the hidden tasks. I call it the "what's NOT in the appointment book" that wins the client over.

I never bothered much with studying the appointment book. For me, it was always a rough guide. People came early. People came late. Their needs differed to those they'd book in for. Sometimes they needed more. Sometimes they needed less. It was always shifting sand. I never panicked; it always worked out in the end. If it hasn't worked out yet, it isn't the end – your client makes another appointment for another day, has another service and then it works out. The end.

The only way to control your appointment book is to personally re-book every client yourself. But we're still dealing with mostly women and we're world champions at changing our minds. You need to go with the flow.

Some of you will be thinking *OMG that's me!* and others *I couldn't work like that, it's way too up in the air for me. I need to stick to the script.*

We all differ in how we approach our day. That's a good thing. The one thing that must remain constant is the result we give to each client. If you're not thinking of the person in the chair beyond this one appointment, you have it all wrong. Solve the problem for her for today AND ongoing. It's NOT about you or the appointment book. Tell your client what she needs this time … and next time.

3

" *Recommending products and services to your clients is a job. Period.* "

Missing any opportunity to wow a client.

If you've read my other books you'll know this story. In 1984 I went into a salon in Melbourne. The way the stylist cared for me that day has never left me. I had short hair back then and wanted desperately for it to be long. That yearning came up in conversation because she asked a bigger question. Bigger than the appointment I was booked in for. She asked me: *If you could have any hair at all, what type of hair would you want?*

3

My curls usually got the better of me. Growing my hair out was difficult as it grew sideways and not down like straight or "normal" hair does. This girl suggested my hair could be blow waved every Saturday morning back where I lived. It would hold for the weekend and help me get past the awkward growing-it-out stage. I left the salon that day with the first shampoo and conditioner I ever bought. It contained wheat germ and was good for blondes (like me). Knowing I lived some 400km away from her didn't stop her making her recommendations.

I did exactly what she said. Every Saturday morning I sat amongst the oldies at Jill's Hair Boutique in downtown Hopetoun and had a blow wave before I headed off to the local football match. I was 19 years of age. For the first time, I grew my hair long and all because the girl in the salon in Melbourne paid it forward. We should all be giving our recommendations like she did that day. She could have judged me on many levels: too young to have a blow wave every week, doesn't have the time, won't spend the money, doesn't live near me so who cares or it's none of my business.

That day was the beginning of my hairdressing career. I've never forgotten the way she made me feel. Do I remember what she charged me? I have no idea. It didn't matter. The way I felt when I walked out onto Elizabeth Street was priceless.

Forgetting to have some fun with it.

Some time back, I worked with a salon owner who was an exceptional product retailer but was struggling because his team was not. This is what I said to him. "Sometimes you just need to have some fun around the basics to get them there. A simple gesture of a glass jar full of chocolate bars could be the energy you need. Why not try it on Saturday." He left our meeting pumped, as you do.

Today, dangling a chocolate bar probably isn't going to work in many workplaces. I've known health-conscious salon teams that have used berries as an incentive – strawberries, blueberries and raspberries. At $6 a pop it's still a win.

This particular salon owner decided to stick $10 notes on his fridge – ten of them. The girls arrived at work that morning and one by one noticed the money on the fridge. We do like a visual! The salon owner explained the rules of the game: anyone who did a basin service that day would get a $10 prize.

Guess what? There was no money left on the fridge at the end of the day. Did that fix the problem long term? No, of course it didn't. But it proved to him and the team that they could do it once they put their minds to it. Even though the only reason the client was getting a basin service treatment on that day was the bonus on offer for the team member. Selfish, I know, but they fell into his trap.

That's why short-term targets don't work other than as an example – a case in point to help you convince your team that when they don't do their job, their clients miss out.

It didn't happen overnight, but we did get the salon's retail sales and basin services to where we wanted them. First we had to change the mindset of the entire team from a selfish viewpoint to that of the client.

Not knowing your products.

Gone are the days of just reading the bottle to gain knowledge of the product. With easy access to the internet and YouTube there's no excuse for not understanding how, what and why you should use a product today. There's so much information out there on what we can do and use with our skin and hair. It's almost overwhelming. Think of this knowledge as the shortcut to what your client wants.

Believing your knowledge doesn't matter.

Imagine you go into the hardware store because you need to paint your decking. You go to the paint section and start looking at all the cans of decking sealers. You read things like *Coverage: 30 square metres* and wonder how much you'll need. You see dozens of tint shades of paint and wonder what colour you need. The next can claims to wash out in water. Do you need water-based or longer wearing oil-based? And look, there's even one for a boat.

That's when most of us go looking for a shop assistant, someone who can solve our problem, eliminate the guesswork and help us make a smart decision. The alternative is to keep reading the product info on the cans. Who's got time to waste like that? Not me. I'm impatient. I'm not the reading cans type. I want the short list. I'd seek help as I entered the store, before I even reached the paint section. It's a girl thing – we like to ask straight up. Men try to work it out and only ask if they get stuck. On average, women live five years longer than they men do. Maybe this is why. (Just saying.)

Even if someone recommended a specific decking finish to you and you have a picture of the can on your phone, you're probably going to need help to work out how much you need, how to apply it and how to maintain it. It's the same in our industry – clients either get a word-of-mouth recommendation or go into a salon and ask for help. Always think about making things easier for your clients –telling them what they need makes it easier for them. Don't make them read the can, so to speak.

3

Whinging about the competition.

I constantly hear complaints about product companies who supply to salons, supermarkets and big warehouse stores. I believe people only buy hair and beauty products from the supermarket because they don't know any better. They don't know any better because we haven't bothered to do our job of educating them.

We need to have a long hard look at ourselves. We make excuses based on our own bias, our own limiting beliefs and our own principles.

The best of the best professional products are sold through professional hair and beauty businesses. We will always be competing with the supermarkets. That's never going to change so you need to get over it and get on with doing your job.

Stocking any old products.

You need to get your head around what you stock and why. If you're like me and wouldn't buy anything that's been tested on animals, then only stock cruelty-free products. That matters to me; it may not be important to you. Maybe you prefer products made in your own country or brands that support a charity or cause. Whatever floats your boat. Just remember to keep your clients' interests front of mind.

3

Natural and organic ingredients are all the go, but are you certain the manufacturers' claims are true given the current regulations? It's a can of worms you may not want to open. Coming from a girl who has Botox (the cruelty-free variety, of course) in her forehead, maybe I'm not in a position to comment. Botox is a botulism-based product that paralyses the muscles so I probably surrendered my rights to preach to anyone on what is or isn't pure.

Having said that, I do practise yoga daily and that's given me an enormous benefit but I'm not quite ready to be a full-blown hippie just yet. I think of myself as a cosmopolitan hippie. You need to accept that your clients may or may not share your beliefs (whatever they may be). You should respect their choices and give them options in terms of price and whether ingredients are natural or not. Try not to push all your beliefs on them; just do your job and let people decide

Flogging a dead horse.

I was in the supermarket and noticed a big sale on Pantene products. Hairdressers hate Pantene in the same way dogs chase cats, and for good reason. I decided to wait and watch to see who was buying Pantene. Soon there were a couple of girls looking at the Pantene and I was tempted to tell them they'd be better off getting professional advice about hair products. Then I noticed their hair. What a disaster. Obviously neither of them valued the look of their hair. One head of hair was bleached within an inch of its life and had more bands than the *Big Day Out*. The other one was layer-upon-layer-upon-layer-upon-layer of black tint. Yuck! I doubt either girl was a regular at a quality salon. I could smell backyard or supermarket colour box hairdressing at ten paces.

My point is this: not everyone wants your information and expertise. Sometimes you'd be wasting your time, flogging a dead horse that was never going to come back to life. These two girls I encountered in the supermarket were never (ever) going to be open to my advice. And they'd be D grade salon clients at best. Your mission is to work on your A, B and C grade clients, wowing them with your professional knowledge and transforming them into A grade clients who rave about your salon.

Thinking it's not your job.

You probably know already that I have this great mop of curly hair. It's my mother's fault. She says God gave us little stomachs and big heads of hair, and she's pleased it wasn't the other way around. So am I.

It doesn't matter where I go someone asks me about my hair. Often it's three times in a day. I'm a walking advertisement for the hair and beauty industry. Just the other day I was in an opportunity shop donating some stuff after a bit of a clean out when a lady commented on my hair. She had curls too and asked what I used on mine. When I told her she wrote down the name of the product and the company name.

I gave her a few tips on how to use the product – like dry it in with a diffuser or it will be crunchy like two-minute noodles – and then I was off. Two weeks later I ran into her at a café. She approached me, reminded me who she was and told me how grateful she was for my help. She'd Googled the product I'd suggested, found a nearby stockist and bought it the very next day. She'd been using it since and asked me how I thought she was going with it. I told her I loved it. This lady was 60 years of age if she was a day. Yes, we all have the resources if we want to learn.

Sadly, that lady had been going to a salon to get her regular cut. It seems that was ALL she was getting. I was the one doing a proper job out on the streets. I don't mind, but her regular hairdresser is missing out on being one of the white horse guys. Perhaps you arc, too?

It's your job to know what products work and who they'll work for.

People want this information and they might as well get it from you. What's stopping you from giving it to them?

3

Kick-arse kick-starter.

Think about WHY you started in this industry in the first place. In one sentence, jot it down on a post-it note and stick it on the fridge for all to see. Invite your team to add their own WHYs to the fridge. This is where your what-to-do story begins.

four

chapter

4

Start where it counts.

Why the hell do we consider teaching someone how to retail to their clients as an add-on? Why isn't it the first thing they learn? We should be teaching our team members how to solve problems (with a product or a service) at the beginning of their careers. We need to embed it into the psyche as part of their core professional knowledge. Let me explain what we do wrong.

We teach based on tasks: to stretch the skin tight when waxing, to hold the spray tan gun at a particular distance from the body, to move the spray gun at a steady pace, to be firm when painting on a regrowth tint. But we don't teach our team how to think for themselves, how to solve a problem for someone. We need to teach people how to fish for problems, how to engage a client and how to use knowledge and initiative to solve those problems. If we could do this one thing, we could turn our industry on its head. It would be a true revolution. The power of empowerment.

We haven't given it enough thought. We know juniors can't do the whole job yet so we let them do the part we can control. We let them help us out a little, just enough that we can keep an eye on them. Juniors are always assisting team members more advanced than themselves, the ones with all the knowledge and all the clients. So why don't we start the serious knowledge transfer earlier? Right at the very start?

4

To get a revolution happening, we need dramatic change. We need to see the value in teaching consultation, problem-solving and active thinking much, much earlier than we do now. Not doing so creates a monster that will bite you on the arse further down the track.

If your team can't engage a client and solve a problem without you looking over their shoulder, they're not able to do their job unassisted. If they can't work unassisted, how will they ever build clientele? You, the salon owner, and any other seniors on your team are forever tied to the client and the business.

And you're sending an unconscious message to your client that this person can assist you but, when it comes to recommending the solution to anything (that is, solving the problem), they're not capable and can't be trusted.

Let's train our people from the start.

Let's teach our industry up-and-comers how to think for themselves, to identify client needs and recommend appropriate solutions. Role-play is a great place to start the education process. Yes, I see you rolling your eyes. Nobody likes role-play. You need to get over that thinking – and fast. Role-play is the only way you can teach problem solving from the get go. You don't even need a model, you just need a picture of something that someone wants to achieve, a desired outcome. It's all about refining and rehearsing how you'd go about the client interaction including a plan for home hair care or skincare.

Retail Sales 101.

I believe "Retail Sales" should be a unit of education to be assessed and passed like any other skill taught in our industry. I've never met a person who's great at retail who's not a fabulously confident all-rounder.

Knowing your product range and how to use it to solve clients' problems gives you enormous confidence. It's a bit "chicken and egg". You need to learn both skillset and mindset problem solving.

If retail was a subject at college, I figure passing would mean being able to consistently recommend retail to every customer with a success rate of 50%, that is, half your clients leaving the salon with a product. If you look after 30 clients a week, you should be getting a hit rate of at least 15 product units a week. If you look after only 10 clients, it still needs to be five products. Easy. If you can't maintain 50%, I suggest you go back to the start and re-learn the process. I know salons that have team members looking after 30 clients a week with a retail strike rate of 25 units a week. It's not a huge stretch to aim for 50% success.

You might be surprised to hear that it's often the quietest team member who does the best recommendations. Sometimes juniors have the most success because their heads are not as full as the seniors; they have less brain distraction or overload.

It's certainly harder to teach an old dog new tricks. I know this because I was the old dog. I'm also proof that with enough drive you can change old habits. Drive is the key. You need to *want* to acquire the skill. I've seen people learn it in a matter of weeks. I've seen others fail to learn it in a matter of months, or worse, years. It's an internal choice. Once you understand that enough micro, inch-by-inch shifts will eventually take you to a different position, you're ready to make the change happen, to see it become an organic part of what you do. That's what I want for you and your team.

The Three Starts.

Here are three small changes you (and your team, even your juniors) can implement tomorrow. They're starter statement's/ questions that shift your mindset to your client needs. I call them The Three Starts.

Start #1
This is what I used on you today.

Too often I struggle to get stylists or beauty therapists to simply show what they used today. Make it your challenge to put every product you use in front of the client and say: *This is what I used on you today.* The simple action of show and tell will change your retail sales. Make it your mission to start tomorrow with: *This is what I used on you today.*

Start #2
What is your biggest challenge with your hair/skin?

We miss this opportunity *all* the time. We get straight to what we're doing today in terms of the service when what we need to do is talk about our client's challenges so we can solve them. Our clients often take things for granted. They don't get that the things they struggle with could be fixed. I've always used lip balms for dry lips without knowing that using a special exfoliate on my lips and a quality, penetrating lip balm would eliminate the dryness. A classic example of solving a problem with product and I'll use that product until a better one is suggested to me.

4

Start #3
How does your hair/skin feel between visits?

Or: *How has your hair/skin been since I saw you last?* Check-in and find out what's been going on since you last saw your client. I don't mean personal stuff. I mean how has their hair been? How has their skin been? That's where you can help them. Ask: *What have you been struggling with?* Understand the behaviour of their skin or their hair. You can solve almost anything with a product. And if you did recommend something last time and they took your advice and bought a product, you need to check-in again and make sure they're still enjoying the benefits. Are they out of it? Do they need any more?

Why do some of your clients buy online?

The same reason we buy anything online – some people find it much easier than hoofing it to an actual store. You need to understand the edge you have over the online store. You offer your client benefits they can't get online: touching the product, opening it and smelling it. If it's not to their liking, they can return the product and talk to you about their experience.

> " *Planning the difference between a **smooth** and a **rough day**, between an average and a **wow** experience.* "

Online is like shopping in a supermarket – it's fine if you know what you want. If you don't know what you want or need, shopping online can be a nightmare. You can read online reviews to the point of total boredom, be confused by the array of products available and be uncertain about identifying your problem in the first place. Or, you can go to your friendly professional at your local salon and get first-hand advice.

I was on a flight recently and the flight attendant was admiring my curls and I said, "Right back at ya!" Her hair was much curlier than mine. She told me about her wonderful hairdresser and his celebrity clientele. He'd been looking after her for several years and she loved her salon visits.

When I asked what products she used, she couldn't remember the name, just that it was extremely difficult to find. I asked about the packaging colour and type and she described it as "a little box like a soap box". I knew straight away she was talking about Kevin Murphy's distinctive packaging. But what really interested me was that she felt the product was hard to find. Anyone in hairdressing knows Kevin Murphy is everywhere. High-end professional salons are big fans of Kevin. I think what she meant was that you don't find it in your local supermarket, and to the consumer that seems a little difficult.

4

What I want to know is why isn't her hairdresser checking before she leaves as to how long ago she bought her products and whether she needs to get them now or next time? After all, that's his job!

The process is easier if you plan it.

Before your morning starts, review your client list and check what they had last time. Write yourself some notes about where they'd likely be up to today with their products. Now you're in a great position to not only show your clients you care about them but to also start a relevant conversation about their problems and product solutions. Do your homework before your client arrives and be ready to give them the best possible salon experience. Planning is the difference between a smooth and a rough day, between an average and a wow-me experience.

Kick-arse kick-starter.

Start with just one. Check the record for your next client *before* they arrive. Know what product you recommended or advice you shared at their last appointment, and refer to it during today's visit. No notes to review? Make up for it ... take notes this time, so you're ready for their next visit. They'll love you for it.

4

five

chapter

Excuse you ...
isn't that BS?

Like everything in life, learning to retail is just another skill. Some people start off with a natural talent for recommending retail. For others it's not such an easy fit. Either way, success depends on you being prepared to learn.

5

Think about this. If you put a bunch of coloured pencils and paper in front of pre-school kids, in no time at all they'll draw. They just get on with it.

If you take the same kids when they're aged 13 or 14 years, some will hesitate and start to tell you they can't draw. During the decade in between, their experiences (good and bad) have shaped them. They've decided, through either failure or success, that they can or cannot draw. And that becomes their reality because they never believe otherwise.

When I'm working with salon team members I come across many people who claim they don't do "this" or they don't do "that". In hairdressing, many claim they don't do hair up. "It's not my thing," they say. What they're really saying is, "I'm not confident". Probably because they didn't stick at it long enough to be good at it. I don't get that type of thinking. It's selfish, unless you work in a very large team where you have specialists in every area. You might have barbers who specialise in men's cutting or you might have guys who are amazing with colour and are genuine technicians. Then there are those who are educated in extensions. The same goes for beauty – there are some girls who won't do needling or triple X waxes. Once again, it's just not their thing. And once again, I'll tell you it's just an excuse and it's more about your own interests than your clients' interests.

5 Five flimsy BS excuses.

Be careful when you make an excuse because some of us can see straight through your BS.

Here are the five flimsiest-of-the-flimsiest excuses I've heard for why you can't recommend retail to your client.

1. My clients already have everything.

2. I don't like this range of products.

3. I forgot.

4. I don't have time.

5. My clients can't afford it

I call BS on all five… here's why.

BS Excuse #1

Your clients already have everything? Really? I bet you $100 I can prove that's not true. All I'd have to do is go to the client history and look at when they last purchased product. Then I'd ask you about a leave-in moisturiser or a heat protector and dry shampoo. That's just the hairdressing version. Skincare version is a much bigger pool to fish in. I'd start with eye cream, sunscreen and serums (there's a whole alphabet of serums, and you guessed it I'm using all of them). Give yourself a reality check. Go to the computer, pick out four of your regulars and see whether "they have everything" is a BS excuse. We both know it is.

BS Excuse #2

You don't like this range of product? That statement is all about you and nothing about your client. If you don't like that product range, then you need to get to know it better and understand its benefits. A poor workman blames his tools. I've walked out of a salon where everyone's whinging about their product range (doesn't sell, too expensive, customer complaints) and straight into the next salon where they're raving about how much they love their range, how it sells itself because it's so fantastic. Same product range, two different salons. Go figure.

Product ranges don't get to the public without big bucks poured into their research and development. If that's the product range you must work with and you are an employee, then get over it … and get on with it. If you're the salon owner and truly believe your product range doesn't work, then go find one that does. If you believe the quality of the product range is holding you and your team back from kick-arse retail, it's up to you to fix it, not use it as an excuse.

BS Excuse #3

You forgot? Pah-lease! Let me ask you this: if a lady were booked in for an eyebrow wax, would it be possible to wax one brow and forget the other brow? No, of course not. That's because the left one is equally important as the right one. The service you provide is not complete without finding out what products are needed to support your work between visits. It's as crucial as doing both eyebrows. The only reason you'd forget is that you don't rate it as important. That's why you're here reading. Keep on reading! I'll convince you just how important retail is.

BS Excuse #4

You don't have time? Let's get something straight – everyone gets allocated the same 24 hours a day. It doesn't matter how clever you are or how much money you have, you still get 24 hours a day. What you're really saying is: *I'm so disorganised and unfocused that I don't make time to recommend products to my clients therefore I'm only doing half the job.* Isn't that interesting? When you tell me you don't have time, that's all I'm hearing – lame excuses. Preparation plus planning is the answer to your time management issues. If you print out your client list for the day, take ten minutes to look at their histories and make a few notes on the side, you'll be ready for your client and ready to change your retail results.

BS Excuse #5

They can't afford it? Where people spend their money is none of your business. Your job is to make sure your clients have knowledge and expert advice, given freely and without judgement. Have you ever been surprised when a client buys a product from you? On the other hand, some people look like they'd spend and yet they're two turns tighter than tight. Either way, it's not your business. Your job is to recommend the right products to the right people, based on their needs, not their budgets. If they choose not to take a product with them, think about offering a sample instead. I used to tell my clients: "If you love this product at $30, it's an absolute bargain. If you hate it, then this product at $30 is a huge waste of money. What I can do for you is give you a sample. Test it yourself at home in your bathroom and you'll soon know if it's right for you. Come back and see me if you love it. It will be written in your notes so, if I'm not in that day, one of the others will know exactly which one you tested."

5

" *If you* **love this product at $30,** *it's an* **absolute bargain.** *If you* **hate it,** *then this product at $30 is* **a huge waste of money.** "

Don't be limited by your beliefs.

Excuses are just that – excuses. They are limiting beliefs and (trust me) I've heard every one of them before. I want you to challenge yourself on what holds you back. People make time to do the things they think are valuable. Think about what's truly valuable to you, your clients and your business.

I'm fascinated by the lengths people go to for things that are important to them, often things I wouldn't even bother with. When I'm out walking my dog early in the morning I quite often see a lady outside the Royal Children's Hospital here in Melbourne. She's living proof to me that everyone has their own set of priorities. Hers and mine couldn't be further apart. This lady looks to be in her mid-fifties and obviously works in the hospital. By her uniform, I guess she's part of the catering team. She comes out the front of the hospital to have a smoke, bringing her own portable fold-up ashtray and a hand towel. She sits on the hand towel, I guess to protect her bum from the cold concrete. My question is: What is she doing to protect herself from getting lung cancer? I'm telling you this because it's a clear case of doing what matters to you. If you've known anyone with lung cancer, you know it's a slow and horrific death you wouldn't wish on your enemy. I've never heard of anyone dying a horrible slow death because of a cold bum. What on earth is she thinking?

We're all different. That's what makes us truly human. But sometimes you've got to give your thinking a critical once-over and decide whether it's based on BS or logic. When it comes

to salon retail, your limiting beliefs are only fooling yourself …
and your clients.

Kick-arse kick-starter.

Think about the last client you looked after. I'm guessing you didn't recommend retail to them? I mean that's why you're here, right? So think about what went through your head, what BS excuse you made to yourself to justify not recommending. Now you see it for what it is, you can change it (next time). You can't change what you can't see.

5

chapter

:six

6

The value of trust (and why it's all about you).

Our industry is changing. We're on the verge of a revolution. I can feel it!

Sitting is now frowned upon. So is sugar. It's just a matter of time before people discover that the way you look on the outside triggers the way you feel on the inside. So many people take anti-depressants today. My sister who is in health care says we should forget fluoride –the government should put Lexapro into our water supply.

I believe part of the solution is people taking more pride in themselves and spending more time in a salon getting spoiled. That's opportunity, right there.

As a true hair or beauty professional, you simply can't get away with not knowing your stuff. The Internet has forever changed the world. People are more informed than ever and they expect expertise and experience. Gone are the days of

6

simply accepting someone's word for what's best for your hair, skin or nails. People want to make informed decisions. As a professional, it's your job to inform them.

I'll tell you a story about my mum and doing what the doctor said was just the "norm". It's hard to believe that such an intelligent, caring and kind woman accepted the doctor's advice without question. I've got five brothers, yet it wasn't until I had my twin sons that I gave much thought to whether we should have them circumcised. The twins' father thought we definitely should not. I wasn't convinced. I started to ask people's opinions and do my own research on the topic.

When I asked my mother about my brothers, her response blew me away. Not only was she unsure about which of her sons were circumcised and which were not, she hadn't given it much thought at all. She said the doctor who took care of her pregnancy and birth of her first couple of children popped his head in her hospital room door one morning and said, "I'll be back later to circumcise the baby."

"Right," she said and then thought: *What is he talking about? What is circumcise?* She asked one of the other new mums, accepted her explanation and that was it – she just took the doctor's word for it. After that doctor retired, she was allocated another one who didn't think circumcision was necessary. Once again, she took his advice on face value.

What I want to know is: Where was my father? I asked her that and she said, "Oh, I can't remember where dad was in the decision-making or whether the first two or three were circumcised and the last two or three were not."

We've come a long way. In today's educated climate, decision-making around circumcision is much more informed. I think circumcising (or not) your son is a huge decision. There's no way that simple acceptance would happen today when people are so aware of their options. In hairdressing or beauty, decision-making is similarly well-informed. If you don't share your knowledge and present yourself as the expert you are, you're letting your clients down. Eventually they'll work that out and go in search of someone who'll give them what they need to make sound choices.

Certain statistics around loyalty and client retention relate directly to retail sales. This is why I bang on about the importance of retail. In my opinion you can get a haircut or facial anywhere. What will set you apart from your competitors is that you go the extra mile and share your knowledge with your client.

6

Clients buy from people they know, like and trust; that's where your focus needs to be.

This truth applies to every person you look after, from first-time clients to those you've looked after since the beginning of time. Every one of them is entitled to your expert opinion. Let *them* choose to act on it or not.

There are two ways to look at everything. To get crystal clear on why you need to recommend retail to both new and existing clients, let's look at them separately.

> ## *"Learn like nobody else so you can live like nobody else."*

Your new clients. Do you choose not to recommend products to new clients because you feel you haven't had a chance to build rapport with them yet? That's a very limiting belief, a myth that we need to bust. That person is new to you because, for one reason or another, they chose not to return to their previous salon. Here's my tip: it's probably because they didn't get the expertise they needed there. Regardless of whether the client is new to you or not, you need to be the expert and share what you know, every time.

Your existing clients. Sometimes, you get so involved in your clients' lives that it becomes more important than the actual task. If so, you're risking not doing your job, not making the professional recommendations you should. When you're too familiar with your clients, you expect them to speak up when their needs aren't being met. A huge mistake! It's your job to ask the questions that will reveal the problems you can solve for them, not the other way around. Be mindful about ratio of personal to professional conversation. It's not easy. They come in ready to tell you their latest life episode. You need to carefully stop them right there. Try this: "I'm dying to hear how the wedding went. Let me first sort out your hair/skin needs, then you can tell me all about it while I look after you."

You're in control and you can never be accused of losing your way. And don't make up your mind about whether or not they'd be interested in purchasing a product before you've even asked. No two visits are the same. Set up your system, follow it and you'll have fresh advice every time.

Clients' trust is huge – grow it, don't blow it.

An American research company came up with these statistics. I find them fascinating because they resonate with what my experience tells me. If a client buys a product from you, they are 30% more likely to return. If a client buys two products, they are 60% more likely to return. And the client who stocks up with three products is 90% more likely to return. Why? That's easy – people buy from people they know, like and trust. There's no way you'd purchase from someone you didn't trust. If you're always thinking about solving problems and genuinely sharing your knowledge, the sale will come.

6

I worked with a laser clinic where the business owner struggled to keep up with the demands of booming retail sales. The girls had engaged my learnings full throttle and the products were literally flying off the shelf. Now, there's a ZING thing … we fix your current problem but we always create you another one, a better one. Leaping from not selling enough to not being able to keep up with your volume of sales is an enviable problem to have!

Initially, team members were low on product knowledge and therefore they lacked the confidence to recommend. After a couple of months of intense training with their product companies, their product knowledge grew, their confidence blossomed and their ability to recommend retail went through the roof. They were off and running.

The next challenge was keeping stock on the shelf. The clinic went from holding about $15,000 in retail stock to almost $30,000 (in heavy-duty beauty, that's not hard to do). They ordered weekly instead of the previous random "whenever" system. Many items sold at over $100 so it takes good money management and planning to stock plenty of what you need.

Because the team struggled with recommending out-of-stock product, we devised a new strategy. If a customer purchased the product and it wasn't on the shelf, the team member took their payment and addressed an "express" postage bag, there and then, in front of the client. As soon as the product re-stocked, it went straight out the door to the customer. They got their product and its benefits fast without having to make a special visit back to the clinic. As the clinic grew, the financial situation improved and it became easier to hold more stock.

The big shift here was the team learning their product range inside and out. There's a saying that goes like this: *Learn like nobody else so you can live like nobody else.* Knowing your stuff and being confident will open doors for you. If you're a team member, you'll get the promotion. If you're the salon owner, serious retail sales can pay for a fabulous holiday every year. The better the sales the better the holiday.

As I said, the second problem was better than the first.

Building trust and rapport.

Have you ever been shopping for clothes and you find something you think you might like to buy? You head into the cubicle and try on the first item. When you emerge to check yourself out in the mirror, you see that you look ridiculous. Right about then the sales assistant comes over and says something only a twit could say, considering the look on your face: "That looks great!"

You're thinking: "You have to be kidding." Now you know she hasn't a clue and you can't take anything she says seriously.

In contrast, a great sales assistant will ask you, "Is there an occasion? Would you like me to help you with anything? I'm here if you need me."

Or maybe: "Okay, so I think I should help you here. What are you looking for? Would you like me to make a suggestion? I could come back with something else, if you like."

I'd be happy with any of those.

After all, she's a sales assistant, which means she's paid to assist you to make a sale. Her caring about your outcome is effortless. She's just doing her job. You sense she is genuine and you start to build rapport. You start liking her, then you start trusting her … and that's when the buying starts. All in a matter of minutes. That's the priceless part of making a sale.

You can help create trust, too. Be honest, don't force it, share your knowledge and show you care. That's how you build rapport.

Kick-arse kick-starter.

Think about the last time you bought a special something at a boutique. Recall how the sales assistant helped or didn't help you. In your head, critique her level of care. Did you trust her? Why or why not? What can you learn from your experience?

6

seven

chapter

Why you should never give up.

You may have noticed we're already at Chapter 7 and I haven't mentioned the financial gain from retail … until now.

If money is the only reason you're reading this book and the only reason you want to learn to recommend products to your clients, then I have news for you. Bad news. It won't last.

I've always believed that being driven by money, and money alone, is not sustainable. At ZING, we teach you that change comes from your mindset. We shift the way you think about your Time, your Team and your Money.

It must be in that order. If you make time to work with your team, the money will show up.

You have to make time to teach your team the skills you *all* need. Yes, I mean you, too! As salon leader, you're the lynchpin in the learning. Do that and I promise you: the money will show up.

The MUM TEST.

Yesterday I asked a salon owner I've been mentoring for maybe 10 weeks: *Why are your team not doing their job?* I just didn't get. We should have been seeing serious change and, apart from the owner herself, there was nothing. If she'd told me her entire team was deaf, it might have made sense because it seemed they hadn't heard a single word she'd said.

I delved deeper. *Why is it that you have recommended retail to your clients and they're taking your advice and buying products, yet your team haven't moved? Don't they care?* One team member had seen 23 people that week and sold not one retail unit. WTF? (Did you notice I didn't say serviced? Because she didn't service them. Not properly anyway.)

I told the owner she had to step up. *You need to go in and say NOT GOOD ENOUGH and ask them if they honestly think this lazy approach is good enough? You need to do the MUM TEST.*

The MUM TEST is this: *If this client were your mother, would you be happy with this level of care for her?* Exactly.

This salon owner was just too lovely and it was costing her hundreds of dollars every week, not to mention the personal toll of feeling both stressed and a failure. Although she'd constantly asked her team to lift their level of service, it wasn't working. We needed a new approach. She had to tell them straight. Once I put it bluntly, she went in and took them on. I hit a nerve when I said: *They're stealing from you, they're robbing you of having the business you deserve and all that comes with it.*

7

Why are you letting them run the show? And an ordinary show one at that.

It could have gone either way. It was a risk I had to take. I can't do my job if the person I'm mentoring doesn't do their job. That's the truth of it. A great coach gets you to do the things you don't want to do so you get the results you do want.

Two days later, the salon owner checked in with me. The team of four had sold 33 basin services and well over $2,000 of retail in the two days. That would normally be three weeks worth for this salon.

Is it a coincidence that everyone just happened to be buying in those two days? Absolutely not. Her team (eventually) did their job. Period.

Selling retail is smart, not hard.

Let me teach you a little about working smart, not hard. If you were to do a men's hair cut, it might take you 30 minutes and you charge $45. Some of you'll be charging $35 and some of you $95. Either way, for this exercise, it's half an hour of your time. If, during that half hour, you were to chat with your client about why he'd be better off using a product that is laurel sulphate free (minimises his risk of baldness) or how finishing with a styling product would help him look his shiny best, he might take one of your recommendations and purchase a $35 product. While you were working on his haircut, you made your best recommendations and so the original $45 sale is now $80. Sure, half the $35 is hard costs but your wages have already been factored into the haircut costs. In reality, half of the product cost is cream on top of your well-iced cake.

Imagine if every one of your clients left with one product. Imagine what that would look like added to your bottom line. I've seen it happen again and again. And it makes me smile every single time I get a thank you text or email boasting about how well the team are going with their retail. Because not only is it an instant financial gain, but I know that you're building trust and loyalty with your clients.

To get real lasting change, make it your priority to listen for the clues to solving clients' problems.

Just keep going.

In a way, this book is no different to a diet book. Yes, it has all the answers and all the solutions but for success, you must make time to implement. That's the tricky part. The reading is the easy part. If you've ever worked with me, you'll have heard me say, "If it was that easy any Joe or Josephine could do it." The first thing you must do is make up your mind that you're going to train the team and never give up.

That might mean some of the people on your team need to find another salon. That's OK. Not everyone wants to play at your level of client care. You need to move the people who are holding you back.

The Crab in the Basket Theory.

Have you heard of The Crab in the Basket Theory? My very first coach Bruce explained this to me and I still use it. It goes like this. If you're at the beach catching crabs and you put one crab in a basket, it will escape. You need to put a lid on your basket to stop the crab climbing out. However, if you put more than one crab in the basket, you don't need the lid. I kid you not! When one crab goes to crawl out of the basket, the other crab or crabs grab him by the leg and pull him back in. It's true. I have no idea why they do it but one crab stops the other crab going places.

We all know people like that, don't we? It's the same for us in life: some people will always be pulling you down, holding you back when you try to achieve something bigger and better, when you try to escape from what you've always done.

All change takes time. Before you begin shifting the thinking about retail in your salon or clinic, take the time to get permission from everyone on your team. You want to hear:

"Yes, we are in! We're ready to make the changes we need so we can all recommend retail and make solving problems for our clients the new norm." (More about that in Chapter 8.)

Prepare yourself. There will always be someone who will tell you your clients don't have the money or that they can get retail cheaper online. Blah, blah, blah …

I used to work with a particular beauty salon owner in Melbourne. Some months after I finished working with her, I started working with a hair salon owner in the same suburb. We decided the rent he was paying was too high and it was time to explore other options. He ended up relocating to right beside the beauty salon I'd been mentoring. It created great synergy – clients going into the beauty salon could now see there was a hair salon right next door.

7

" *Not everyone* wants to play at *your level of client care.* "

The beauty salon was okay at retail but had never mastered it as consistently as I'd have liked. The owner was great but her team let her down. One day I took a call from her. She whispered to me that she had some information she thought I might like to know – that all her clients were telling her about next door.

"It's terrible, they're shoving products down people's throats."

So I whispered back, "Really? Just so I'm clear, every one of your customers is complaining?"

"Every one," she replied. "Well, not every one, but a lot."

"A lot?" I asked. "So, can you name ten of them?" Of course, she couldn't. She could name two, because there were only two.

This is what I whispered back to her: "Your team can't recommend retail to save themselves. So perhaps the team member who came to you with this wild accusation is actually the crab in the basket. She's pulling down anyone else who's succeeding, even if they're in the business next door. There are more than 100 clients a week going through the hair salon next door. If only two have mentioned they don't like the way they're being recommended hair care, I'm OK with that."

Her information had come from a team member who was a notorious gossip. I recommended the beauty salon owner tell the gossip to mind her own business, put her energy into recommending products to her clients and stop worrying about what they're doing next door.

She burst out laughing. "Why didn't I see what was going on?"

"I don't know," I replied. "Now get back to work." She hung up the phone laughing. She knew she should have known better. I loved working with this client; she was hilarious. I used to spend half my time keeping her on track.

The trouble with our industry is: there are more people in the sales prevention department than the actual sales department. Be wary of them.

There will always be someone out there telling you it can't be done. All you need to do is keep away from them and remember The Crab in the Basket Theory.

Kick-arse kick-starter.

Go make yourself a cuppa, sit down and think about all the times you've had a great idea and someone's talked you out of it. Is it time you told them The Crab in the Basket Theory?

7

eight

chapter

Telling not selling, from day one.

Starting tomorrow, make a key change in your business. Make a promise to yourself that you'll always start training retail from the start. With *every* new team member who joins your salon. Tell them upfront: *We're a strong retail salon. We're going to teach you the same system we use.*

Get their permission to train them, there and then. Why? Because in the beginning they'll agree to it. Each new team member has an attitude like a martini glass: a very wide opening at the top where it counts. It's easy to get information in. They say YES a lot.

8

Down the track they tend to get lazy. No, not all of them, but lots of them take their position for granted. They change from resembling a martini glass to being more like a champagne flute – very narrow at the top (with thinking to match).

Retail training is not an add-on. Always begin it early.

Why retail is like your sex life.

With new or existing team members, your secret to success is making the concept of recommending retail exciting. Explain you'll be patient with them if they follow your system and that you understand it might take some time to get it right.

Your retail is no different to your sex life.

You might be thinking: *What the hell does salon retail have to do with my sex life?*

Most people try retail and when they don't get it right first time, they never think it'll improve. At the risk of over sharing, I can tell you I've been practising (both retail and sex) for years and I'm still getting better. I bet you're enjoying yours more now than when you first began. LOL.

Nobody ever says, "Hi, my name's Barry. I'm not that good at sex." So why should you do the same for your salon retail?

Good retail is the same as good sex. You need to keep at it, explore new ways to do the exact same thing, and don't be fooled into thinking you're too old, past it or can't be bothered anymore. See, I told you it was the same as your sex life. Don't be so lazy, people! Put your back into it and you'll get much more out of it. The rewards are huge (in both camps).

Tell don't sell.

Just so we're clear: we don't sell people things we tell them what we know, the information that will help them in between salon visits. It's your job to check on things – all the things. *What hairbrush are you using? What brushes are you using to apply makeup at home? What about your hair dryer? How long have you been using that exfoliating mitt I suggested last time? You can look ten years younger when you don't have dark circles under your eyes. Have you thought about using an eye cream?*

We take for granted that the average Joe or Josephine knows about all these things. They don't! You need to check in with them, share what you know. I don't mean share it once. I mean share and repeat, share and repeat, share and repeat, over and over.

Years ago, I did some cross promotion with a beauty salon and insisted that Jane, the owner, come into my salon and have her hair done. I wanted her to experience first-hand how great my team were. I wanted her to know plenty about my salon when she was recommending us to her loyal clients. We did Jane's hair and she was very happy and, of course, wanted to reciprocate. It made sense that I knew more about her salon, too. I headed over to Jane's salon on a busy Friday afternoon. Traffic was horrendous and I got to thinking: *What am I doing? I don't have time for this.* But I'm a girl of my word and I didn't want to let Jane down with a last minute cancellation, so I kept making my way to her salon.

The salon was beautiful, lovely and clean, and it smelt divine – all the things you'd expect from such a polished girl as Jane. My appointment was with Sinead, a beautifully spoken Irish lass. She could tell by my face that I'd climbed four hills and

8

fought off eight tigers to get here (maybe a slight exaggeration). Without me saying a word, she settled me down nicely and in no time I'd forgotten all about the hills and the tigers.

Sinead just went about what she did best: her job. She asked me lots of questions and then she asked me if I had any questions for her, about anything beauty related at all, from hair removal to Botox. She told me now was my chance; she could answer any of my questions.

I immediately sensed I was in the hands of an expert. She explained that the one facial she was going to do today was a great place to start, but what I needed was a plan for my skin and she was happy to help me out. She hoped to educate me around looking after my skin now, so that it continues to look like it does in decades to come. She said there are some services here that can reverse the ageing process. Now she had my attention – any sentence in beauty with the word "reverse" in it has to be a good thing, right? Even better if it also includes "prevention". I love both those words.

8

On Sinead's advice, I took home a couple of products and agreed to buy a pack of six treatments (they were more affordable in a package). What I loved the most about my visits in the next few months was how they made me feel. I work hard, always have, and visiting Sinead every few weeks helped me feel like I was getting a reward for my hard work.

As a hairdresser, I didn't feel spoilt when I had my hair done. This was different. I enjoyed being pampered. It was the beginning of me understanding the real difference between supermarket rubbish and high-end beauty products. I've never looked back.

Sinead never sold me. She told me what she knew and with that information I decided to buy. That's what a true professional does.

People love to buy things.

We buy products to solve problems. If your clients aren't getting their hair and beauty products from you, they're getting them somewhere else. Trust me. Why not make it easier to buy from you? You, the expert who can guide them to making the best choice for their needs.

"Good retail is the same as good sex."

I'm in Bali and my suitcase isn't bulging with clothes. It's brimming with the things I need for my skin, my hair and my health. I'll list a few of my favourites here. Every one of them was a recommendation from either a hairdresser a beauty therapist, a doctor, a naturopath, an advertising campaign or a friend. Either way, it was a suggestion or a recommendation from someone.

These are just a few of the things I brought with me (I have many, many more at home): Dettol Original Hand Soap,

8

Pain-Away Balm, mosquito repellent cream, mosquito repellent spray, Nivea Body Lotion, Aspect Moisturising Cream, PPS Sculpt It, 12 snag-free hair ties, Diflam Plus sore throat lozenges, Revlon Colourstay Lipstick, Mecca Cosmetics Sunscreen 50+, Systane Lubricant Eyedrops, Histoire d Eau de Toilette, Aldi Sunscreen SPF 50+, Ultra A Skin Perfecting Serum, Even Skin Tone Serum, Ultra Replenishing Mask, Frank Body Lip Balm, ALC acetyl l-carnitine, Listerine Pocket Pack, Sue Nicholls SPF 50+, Oral B Super Floss, Ultraceuticals Ultra B Hydrating Serum, Ultra C10+, Ultra Hydrating Milk Cleanser, IntraCeuticals, Napoleon Eye Cream, Banana Boat Halt Protect Face SPF 50+, GC Tooth Mousse, Whispers Makeup Pads, Neutrogena Oil-free Eye Makeup remover Pads, Ombre Cooling Sunscreen SPF 50+, Colgate Total Toothpaste, Betadine Sore Throat Gargle, Napoleon Mosaic Blush, False Lash Superstar Mascara, Extreme Three Razor, Super Stay 24 Colour Lipstick, Napoleon Lip Gloss, Eyelash Curler, Awaphu Replenishing Shampoo, Awaphu Replenishing Conditioner, Repair Keratin Intense Treatment, UltraCeuticals Enzyme Exfoliate, Copper Shampoo and my scratching mitt.

And I haven't even dipped into my makeup bag yet.

I think you get my point. People love buying products.

Kick-arse kick-starter.

Unzip your makeup bag. One at a time, pull out every product and think about where and when you bought it. What made you decide to buy it? What benefits does it give you? How do you know about those benefits? Did someone you trust recommend the product to you?

8

nine

chapter

In your crosshairs – what to aim for.

In this chapter, I'll explain what to aim for when it comes to your retail sales – what's realistic and what's achievable when you have a clear focus.

I've identified a common pattern across salons I work with. Knowing the pattern, I can now guess a salon's retail numbers with very reasonable accuracy within our first 15-minute phone conversation.

The standout constant is the salon owner thinking their retail is higher than it actually is. That's why I bang on about getting the statistics out of your computer and handwriting them into a weekly check-in sheet. Then the numbers sink in.

9

When team members hit their target once they tend to think they hit it all the time! Once is not often. It's once.

Consistent retail sales come from consistent client engagement.

The thing holding salon owners back from retail sales is the same thing holding them (and you) back in general. It's affecting your business and your bottom line.

Client engagement means a consistent loyal clientele. Combine that with basic business smarts and you're well on your way to having the salon business you only ever dreamed of.

I've always felt a strong connection between a salon's culture and customer loyalty. Salon owners come to us for many reason, most put their hand up for help in one area or another. It could be help finding staff. It could be that the owner's exhausted and feels she's the only one doing all the work, that if she physically isn't on site encouraging the team to do their job, it doesn't happen, engagement isn't there and the figures drop.

When your engagement is missing in action, so are your retail sales. Yes, it's that black and white. It's why I won't let engagement (or retail) go when I'm coaching a salon and their team to be the best version of themselves.

9

Retail sales figures have always been a measure of ours at ZING. When we're talking amongst the coaches about a salon, one of the first things we brag about is their retail sales. Why? Because that instantly tells us where the team's at, where they started when we met them and where they are now. It's a way of measuring the care factor. In other words, it shows whether "they give a shit".

Your retail sales figures show whether you give a shit.

Hairdressing salons, beauty salons, spas and medical clinics are all different when it comes to retail. In simple terms, the higher-end clinics have stock that is also at the higher end. Having said that, I've seen great results in all businesses – high-end, budget and everything in between.

It's all about who's leading the team, their beliefs and their ability to educate. Being a great operator is one skill. Running a business with a team is a whole other ball game. Most of you are doing it without ever having learnt how. That was me too – I was off and running the day I opened the door without so much as a simple plan.

Most of you are running a business without ever having learnt how.

I coped by just fixing stuff when it went wrong. It's funny to think back on it now, but that's what I did. Sometimes I fixed the same thing a hundred times! Madness at its best (or worst).

In hairdressing, wherever your retail figures sit now, we can reasonably target to add another 10 units per stylist per week. And I mean *every* week. When I get the stats from salons interested in having us mentor them, most come under 10 units per week. We commonly see 6, 7, 2 and, sometimes, 0 units per week.

9

Once we engage your team – which can take some time depending on how focused you are – we can almost always add another 10 products per week to every team member.

So, 6 becomes 16, 7 becomes 17 and the 2 is now 12. It might not happen overnight, but it will happen.

Have you noticed I talk in terms of product units rather than dollar values? That's for two reasons. Firstly, I want to teach you around problem solving for clients. If you're giving me a figure of $544 or $312, I can't tell what that comprises. Perhaps you've sold one straightening iron for $312, which is one problem solved for one person, or perhaps you've sold 10 x $30 products by solving problems for 10 clients.

"Most of you are running a business without ever having learnt how. "

Focus on the system.

Some of your team have such serious blockages around retail sales, it turns into a tough gig. Many fire off excuses why they're not recommending or simply claim that no one is buying (just another excuse). It's like fishing – if no one's biting, you get a better fishing rod or better bait, right? Same in the salon. You need to look at the effort, refine your technique, and think about what you're doing. You need to get serious about it.

When you start to focus on retail, you'll find the changes start to happen. Numbers often spike upwards after a coaching session then sadly dip back down again. That's OK. You haven't quite got it yet. You just have to keep at it. Retail is like every other skill you learn: practice makes perfect. Think of the hours you've put into cutting hair, over and over until you're confident.

Sometimes, when we shift the coaching to another aspect of the business needing improvement – like developing a training plan for each team member, maybe a marketing campaign or even basin services – we find the retail performance drops off. It's as though the team can only focus on one thing, that juggling more than one ball is too much. That's OK, too. You just need to regroup, refocus and go back to the system you committed to following.

Without a system, there's no way you'll be consistent. It's so important, I'll say it again: without a system, your retail sales will be inconsistent. Period. Getting that into your head is the tricky part. And that's often when the biggest BS excuse of all emerges: *I'm busy being busy.*

To change anything, you need to have a clear picture of what your goal looks like, rather than what you don't want it to look like. In other words, be motivated by the thing that you do want.

9

Think about what it would mean to you to be ordering stock every week because it flies off the shelf. What if you were to lift your retail by $800 a week? (You can, even in a smaller team-of-three salon.) That would mean $400 a week in your pocket after stock costs. If you put that money to the side each week, in a year you'd have around $20,000 – enough to fund an amazing holiday. Why not think about where you'd love to go and make that your focus? Change your phone screen saver to a picture of New York or stick one on your fridge and call it *My Retail Escape Holiday.*

Maybe you dream of paying down your mortgage or credit card debt. It's your money and it's your choice. Just make it your focus and transfer the money to an offset account where you can't easily withdraw it. Now we're talking.

Certain brands attract certain people.

I notice that salons in shopping centres do a lot of retail over the counter, meaning that people just walk in and ask for a particular product. They do this because the team at their regular salon (maybe yours) is forgetting to check how they're going with their products. You do all the educating and another salon gets the sale. Not very clever, is it? Once again, if you have a solid system in place, no one on your team will ever forget to check.

Big global brands can attract clients to your store and also prospective team members who want to work with those brands. Good operators often prefer the products they were trained in and will do their best work where they can use them to solve their clients' problems.

Stocking a brand no one's heard of means you must educate every team member that comes into your business from scratch. Having them arrive with existing knowledge of the product range you stock is a wonderful bonus. It means they settle in fast and hit the ground running when it comes to recommending. Win, win for all.

Baby beauty retail.

The only way I know to describe lower-end beauty is "baby beauty". I'm referring to beauty salons doing waxing, spray tans, manicures and pedicures, some spa treatments and massage, maybe lashes and the odd makeup.

Retail is trickier in baby beauty, especially if 80% of your work is waxing. There are very few relevant products to recommend to your clients. Exfoliating mitts, after-tan products and the odd cuticle oil. And these products are usually infrequent purchases. I've got a cuticle cream I love but I've had it for three years now!

Makeup, on the other hand, offers you more opportunity. I can't tell you how many things I have in my makeup kit! If you have people on your team who love makeup, the products will virtually walk out the door.

Makeup is also a fabulous way to gather an after-hours crowd to your business. Bubbles and a makeup lesson will attract most girls (and some boys, too).

9

I realise for most you, makeup application will be only a small portion of your services. You can invest lots of dollars to fill shelves with product that sits and gathers dust. It's one of the big challenges of baby beauty. As is delivering services in beauty rooms away from where the product is displayed. If you don't have the products with you in your room, ready to easily show your clients, the moment has gone and your clients are more likely to leave without their problem solved. And you're less likely to make a sale.

The number of units being sold in a baby beauty salon can make up as little as 10% of total takings. Often, your girls will touch a lot of clients. Sixty or more people might jump up onto that waxing bed in any given week. At best, they might sell 6 products a week. Are they missing opportunities? Yes, they are. But they also have to work flat stick to service that volume of clients.

Perhaps you can explore other ways to recommend products, maybe around skin care? Or you can introduce other services and move away from this business model into one that offers more opportunity?

Retail in heavy duty beauty.

Heavy duty beauty is the land of opportunity when it comes to recommending retail to your clients. How do I know? Because I'm your target market. I personally use A, B, C and D creams or serums on my face. I joke that every night I wear an alphabet to bed.

The potential here is almost limitless, yet there are still challenges in many clinics and they're often to do with blockages.

One common challenge is the therapist's belief that their client has already spent big dollars on the service and will not be keen to drop another $200 on product.

> **"** *It's so important,* *I'll say it again:* **without a system, your retail sales will be inconsistent.** *Period.* **"**

Retail in heavy duty beauty can easily make up 40% of total takings. The range of relevant products is staggering and clients are often in the 30-plus demographic, where there's often more disposable income.

I'm unsure of the exact figure I've spent on my skin care range to date. Suffice to say, if my house was broken into, I'd prefer the robber to take my TV and leave my skin care behind. I don't watch much TV anyway and keeping my skin care up-to-date is a considerable investment I happily make because I see the results.

If you believe your clients would be better off with home care in the way of products – and who doesn't? – you'll not only get results, you'll get them consistently. Your A grade clients want your expert advice. They're craving it!

9

Here's an example. I started coaching a salon with a team of 10. Eight of them had typically average retail sales. Very average. The other two had great figures, one of them exceptional. She worked about three days a week and typically looked after

18 clients over the three days. She was a colourist and very good at what she did. Of those 18 clients, about 16 of them had a basin service in any given week. Plus she consistently recommended around 20 products a week.

When I quizzed her about her retail being very high, she snapped my head off before I could finish the sentence. She later told me she thought I didn't believe her. Once she calmed down she realised I was in awe of what she could achieve week in, week out.

Her response was priceless. She said, "I'm sick of people thinking I shove products down people's throats. I don't. I would never do that, but it doesn't make sense to me to not make sure they look after their hair at home. If I'm the specialist that I am, then I should do that, right? I'm very good at what I do. My clients travel for miles to have me sort out their colour disasters from people who are just guessing, and there are plenty of salons out there guessing. I tell them upfront and I tell them straight that if they think I'm going to fix their hair here and let them go home without the right home care and ruin it, then it's a waste to give me their money. I don't want it."

How's that for balls?

She said, "I tell them upfront that if you want to look like the girls in the glossy magazines, it's a partnership. I work on you here and I tell you how to look after it between visits using my products. That way you will never find yourself in this mess again."

Listen to that confidence. Wouldn't you sit up and take notice of her, too?

> **Kick-arse kick-starter.**
>
> See your goal. Do a quick calculation for your salon. If you were to add 10 product units per team member per week, how many dollars would that put in your pocket over a year? What would that money mean to you?

9

ten

chapter

Let's lock this shit down.

Have you read enough to know retail is where you need to focus next? Are you convinced that retail is so much more than the dollar amount, it's all about the client engagement? Then let's do this. Let's lock this shit down!

Before you strut back to your salon full of excitement, guns blazing and come off all preacher like, let's get you a plan. The worst thing you can do is blow your team's hair back with well-meaning but ad hoc enthusiasm and demands like: *It's now, it's urgent! You must! Things must be done differently from today!*

First things first. Sit down with your team members one at a time. Maybe buy them a coffee and explain that you're going to make some changes in the way the salon services clients. Ask them for their support. Notice: I didn't say, "Tell them they must join you". Instead, I want you to ask for their help. There's a massive difference.

10

The sun and wind story.

I saw this on a kids' program about twenty years ago when my kids were kids. It was just the lesson I needed to learn at the time. My twin boys were about two years of age and I had to work out how to get them to do things my way and fast. They were both (and still are) headstrong. Maybe they got that from their father. Maybe not.

The story talked about the sun and the wind having a friendly competition, like a dare.

They were hanging about up there in the sky, bored as you might imagine, when the sun said to the wind, "I bet you I can get the coat off that chap walking on the street and you can't".

"You're on," the wind said and insisted he went first.

The wind blew and blew as hard as he could and the man held on to trees and park benches to stop himself from falling over from the terrific sudden winds, but the wind couldn't get his coat off no matter how hard he blew. Eventually he gave up.

Then it was the sun's turn. "Watch this," he said. The sun began to shine and shine until the temperature got hotter and hotter, so much so that the man on the street willingly took off his coat. End of story.

The lesson? Things don't often work as well with force; most things work better if you engage people by shining on them. Likewise, you must be patient with your team and think outside the square to get the results you seek.

I'm thinking that story must have been based in Melbourne. Where else would that type of weather pattern be the norm? In Melbourne, we change the weather sometimes up to four times a day just to please everyone, or maybe it's the sun and wind mucking about up there at our expense. Either way, it's a story I share all the time with my coaching clients. Don't get me wrong – I'm all for GSD (Getting Stuff Done). But I learnt the hard way you have much more success if you have a plan.

I'd like you to get permission from everyone on your team. Ask them to commit to being on the same page as a group. Then you can workshop how your salon's retail system is going to look, function and perform. I know this is your best chance to succeed. When it comes to retail sales the salons that setup simple systems and stick to them are the ones with rockstar results.

10

Get these basics right.

Any plan sits over the top of some serious groundwork. As salon owner, it's up to you to lay solid foundations to help prevent your plan crumbling away. Try these basics for starters.

1. Connect with your rep. Make certain you have all your bases covered by ringing your product company representative. Tell them you're about to make big changes and you'd like their support to educate the team further. Let them in on what you're planning to do. You'll be surprised how supportive a great product rep can be.

2. An agreement in place. Get your team's permission in writing. Make it serious so everyone feels committed. Put together a sentence or two to capture the spirit of the change and have everyone sign off on it.

I agree that, from this day forward, I am going to learn what I need to learn about the products we stock and I am going to share that knowledge with my clients. So they have the best opportunity to manage their hair or skin between visits. Keeping trade secrets is a thing of the past. I will follow the system we come up with together, even when I am under the pump, until it becomes the norm (second nature even).

3. Be fully stocked. Make sure you are fully stocked. When you or your team members go to recommend something, you need to have it in stock. There's nothing worse than not having what you recommend. If you want the team's respect, stock all the products and make it your business to never be out of stock.

10

4. Price every product. I suggest you price-sticker every single product. Source (or print off) some stickers with your logo and the price, to make a clear connection between your brand and the product.

5. Download and learn your products. Log on to www. zingretailresources.com.au for my *Learn Three Products* document. Get the product knowledge you need. You'll never be confident unless you know your products inside and out. Start immediately. All of you. Everyone on your team. Your product representative will be happy to help train you up (more about that in Chapters 18 and 19).

6. Test knowledge and train in the weak spots. You need to test your team on their product knowledge. Confidence comes from knowledge. Your team won't sell a product they don't know everything about. Educate them, test them and test them again. People buy honesty and confidence.

7. Make a system. Make it a system that works for you, not some generic template you picked up from some obscure place. Engage your team in the process of shaping your system. If you do it together, you'll have more team buy-in … and a superior system.

At ZING we take each salon's specific needs into account when we're setting up a system for a team. There are certain common elements (the must-haves) but the rest is shaped by the personality and objectives of the salon owner, the size and nature of the team, the clientele type and a raft of other factors.

10

Retail is my favourite subject. I coach every day (often all day) and I know what works (and what doesn't). My dog Muriel can recommend retail (well, she could if she worked in a salon) – she's listened in on so many lessons. Just like my last dog could have cut hair, she sat in on so many training nights.

You need to appreciate that the skill of selling retail is not learnt overnight. It takes practice and repetition. My top tip here is to encourage the effort rather than the results. Always.

One in, all in.

You need everyone on your team to agree to support one another. No one is going to laugh at someone's attempt or average result. And no one is going to get bigheaded about their success either. You'll need to address the amount of talking each team member does that's not related to doing their job. Sometimes I feel like screaming at the top of my lungs, "Please shut up and do your job! Telling someone about your holiday and your boyfriend is NOT doing your job."

The Squeeze.

Of course, you can't go screaming at people. And you might have a problem with your team retention if you do. That's why I developed another little trick I call The Squeeze.

If someone on your team is waffling on and generally making a short story long, simply walk past them and squeeze their arm. Not hard, just enough for them to get the message. No one other than that team member will know you've even done it.

10

It's a simple reminder to shut up and get on with the job.

What your system needs to include.

1. Start with problem solving. There are many questions that will open this dialogue between you and your client. Make time to gather a few conversation starters, one from each team member. What's their opening question? Mine was always: *What would you want your hair to do, if I had a magic wand? More X? Less Y?* Beauty teams might have similar ideas, depending on the services offered.

2. Always start with moisture, rather than style. That's for hair folks, and for beauty it will be different as there are so many services (more than I can add in here). The principles are the same; they are mostly around the behaviour of the skin.

3. Putting products (unopened ones) in front of your clients. ALL DAY, EVERY DAY.

4. Showing and telling (see Chapter 2).

5. Everyone leaves with either a product or a sample.

6. Asking before you get to the end of the service: *Did you want to take X and Y with you today or just X?* It's never OK to say: *Are you right for products?* while standing at the desk settling the account. That's way too late. The horse has bolted; your client's mind is already on the car, the kids and where she needs to be next.

Walk a mile in each client's shoes.

Then always lead with suggestion.

Imagine not having the tools you need. Imagine if you didn't have the hairdryers, the brushes and all your favourite products. Imagine trying to put your makeup on without your professional brushes. Imagine using your fingertip or those stupid little applicators that come with the makeup. They're impossible to use.

Imagine the difficult position you put your client in when you don't recommend the right tools for them to look after their hair or skin at home. They don't have a third the talent you do so they rely even more on using the right tools and products for the job.

If you don't check, they mostly have shitty tools and substandard products. How's that working for them? Exactly it's not. Understand that when you don't check on what they're working with, you're being mean and selfish. It's not really looking after your clients, is it?

Don't tell me you just want to care for clients. That's the biggest crock of BS I've ever heard.

If you care you will make it your business to share.

10   **Showcase your knowledge.**

Earlier I was telling you about this fabulous product company representative who started to look after me in my first salon. We often had a coffee and a catch-up on industry business.

You can feel isolated as a salon owner, especially a country one. He was great at putting me in the picture of what was going on in the big smoke, which I liked very much.

" Encourage the effort rather than the results. Always. "

One day he told me about salons in the city doing styling nights and how it was creating a great energy in their salons. These styling nights were a good way to build up a junior stylist.

I always felt strongly about educating clients between visits so I thought it was a great idea and worth a shot. Creating a casual and private environment appealed to me.

By then I was no longer working the full five days a week and was thinking about cutting back to two. My aim was to completely get off the floor. I had a fabulous third-year apprentice who was keen to get her hands on as many clients as she could. I said to her, "What if you and I do a styling night together and see how it goes?"

She was keen as mustard, so we invited six of our clients (we only had six chairs back then). We sold them a ticket each for $20 and made that redeemable on products purchased on the night.

10

When they arrived, we shampooed their hair for them then set them up with the tools they needed to style their own hair using a dryer or the GHD irons. Either way, we guided them. It was funny to see – most of them had to stand up to style their hair, they couldn't sit and style. We showed them what we'd do, and let them do it for themselves.

We sold sectioning clips to everyone. I hadn't thought about people trying to manage without them before. We were busy with lots of laughs and lots of product sales being made, along with hairdryers, GHD irons and brushes. Most nights we took between $400 and $600. It was easy and super fun.

Not bad for 90 minutes with your favourite clients. It was the talk of the town. Everyone was saying how cool we were. I loved showing our clients what I knew and it built enormous confidence in my third-year apprentice. She learnt that she already knew a lot more than our clients and it was just a matter of her being in a comfortable environment. She realised that watching and helping was the reason we joined this mad profession in the first place. It was a win for everyone!

Kick-arse kick-starter.

Start with one. Arrange a coffee catch-up with one team member and tell them your plans. Explain what's in it for them, and for you. Ask for their support and listen to their ideas. Really listen. Tick. Now repeat.

10

eleven

chapter

Benefits versus ingredients.

Let's talk about what's inside. I don't mean what's inside your head or your stomach. I mean what's inside the bottle, the actual ingredients.

You might have heard me say, "I don't care what the ingredients are". That statement's only partly true and, more than anything, it comes from a place of frustration.

Rather than the ingredients, I'm more concerned about the benefits of using a product. That's how you'll get me interested, then I might care about the ingredients.

What will the benefits be to your client in using this product (or any of the products you recommend)? That's often the part we miss all together or skim over. And it frustrates me no end.

The ingredients are key, otherwise the product won't deliver. Do you need to know them? Arguably, yes. But foremost you must know the product benefits. Inside and out. Like the back of your hand.

11

What's in it for your client? What result can they expect to achieve if they take your advice today and begin using this product?

And, yes, some people will want to know the ins and outs of the ingredients and you need to respect that, too. But always begin with the benefits. Always.

Choose your battles.

I live in Victoria, Australia. This is a heavily regulated part of the country often referred to as "the nanny state". Sometimes it's like having your grandmother watch over everything you do. Because we are so heavily regulated, I feel I can relax knowing that someone else is checking the ingredients. True or not true, that's how I feel. There are people out there who'd be horrified that I'm so relaxed about something so important. I get that, I just fight other battles that are dearer to me, like teaching you about the importance of retail sales.

What's in it for me?

When you tell someone that a particular skincare product contains seaweed extract, you're only giving value to the person who knows what seaweed extract is and what it does. Instead, you could say, "Have you heard about the recent benefits people are getting using seaweed extract?" If they answer YES, then you could say, "Fabulous! This product is 3% seaweed extract, where most of them are only 1%." That particular client could be very excited about that.

If your client says NO (that they don't know about seaweed extract) then it's your job to explain about seaweed extract and why it's important to use this product containing 3% instead of the usual 1%. Unless you scratch a little deeper and find out if your customer knows or cares about the 3% or 1% and then bother to tell them the benefits, it's of little use. If someone came to me and started telling me about seaweed extract I'd say, "Yeah, that's great, but what's in it for me?"

Each of your clients is different and you need to understand you can't be all things to all people. What you need to do, to be doing your job well, is tell everyone what you recommend for them and why they should be using each product.

Lumpy mail.

I used to send mail-outs to potential ZING clients using a method called lumpy mail. We don't do that anymore because ZING has grown so much so that customers find their way to us by other methods – via my books, my stage presentations for product companies or word-of-mouth. When I was building my business we physically door-knocked and posted out invitations for people to chat with us.

I'd post out our brochure with a note and a coffee sachet (one of those just pour on the hot water and stir type things). The plan with lumpy mail is to have the potential client curious enough to open it (that's why it's called lumpy mail). My note invited the recipient to pour themselves a cuppa and read the information.

It just so happened that on one occasion I sent my lumpy mail to a friend of the owner of a beauty clinic I was mentoring at the time. Word got back to me that she wasn't at all impressed with my lumpy mail-out. You see, her salon was an organic salon and she felt that I should have done my homework and NOT sent her rubbish like that (meaning the Nestlé instant coffee I'd sent).

So, I went to an organic supermarket and spent $10 on a whole box of organic teabags that came in a recycled cardboard box bearing a message that a portion of the purchase price would even go towards saving a goat in a far off land. It was the greenest box of teabags I could get my hands on.

" *Respect everyone else's version of the world* "

I posted them to the salon owner with a note apologising for my misunderstanding. I did so because she had a point. Her salon's name included the word "organic" – she was right to say I'd missed the mark. My point is that the ingredients mattered to her big time. Shampoo and conditioner ingredients would matter a lot to this woman.

I never heard from her. Ingredients were obviously a big deal to her (perhaps even a deal breaker). Communicating is a bigger deal to me. If the roles were reversed, I'd have called and thanked her for the effort made to right the original wrong.

You need to know your audience. If you also feel strongly about the ingredients, you will attract a like-minded clientele.

Just remember that doing something similar (promoting yourself as an "organic" salon) is very niche – it could narrow down your pool of potential clients or act like a beacon lighting the way for those who feel the same way you do. It's an approach with both advantages and challenges. For the salon owner I mentioned, I just hope her product recommending conversations include, "This product is 100% organic which means the benefits to you are X, Y and especially Z."

It's all about respect.

Buying into people's beliefs can be tricky at best. It can go either way. People often say one thing and act in another. Years back, solariums were everywhere and we all used them without much thought of the dangers. It was a lot like smoking cigarettes; nobody made you feel like a leper. Sadly, back then I did both!

I'm way more conscious of my health now. Maybe we're all better informed or perhaps I'm getting smarter in my old age. Maybe it's both.

One day there was a girl paying for her haircut in my salon as another had just finished her solarium session and was having her loyalty card stamped. When the solarium girl left, the haircut girl started ranting about the health dangers of solariums. When she finished having her say, she picked up her pack of cigarettes and stormed off.

I didn't say a word.

I remember the first time a client told me she was pregnant and that she wouldn't be having her hair coloured until after she'd both had the baby *and* stopped breast-feeding. I hope my thoughts didn't reflect on my face because I was thinking WTF!

I'd never heard such a thing and it's certainly different today. I'll never forget my mum's advice to me on motherhood: "Remember who was here first. Children thrive when you, the parents, are happy." I wouldn't be happy if I didn't colour my hair for a year or two. I'd be grumpy for sure.

My point is, that everyone's beliefs are different. You must respect your clients' choices.

We're all different, yet we need to live alongside each other. Just respect everyone else's version of the world.

Kick-arse kick-starter.

From your product shelf, choose a product that's known for its "miracle" ingredient. Using the info sheet or product company's website, work out the product's key benefits. Now, craft a "recommending script" for that product, focusing on the benefits.

twelve

chapter

12

The show must go on.

Working in a hair or beauty salon, dealing face-to-face with clients, is a lot like acting in a play. It's a live performance, where every day is a little like Broadway.

For many of you, having to be "on" or "performing" all day is way too much pressure. Sadly, it's a big reason people leave our industry.

There many more of you in your 20s, than there are of you in your 30s, 40s and 50s. There are two reasons: the physical wear on our bodies is taxing and we are mentally worn out from acting in an endless play, a quite repetitive play at that.

Imagine if you were playing the role of Cinderella in *The Story of Cinderella*. Perhaps you're thinking, "Play it? I am Cinder-bloody-rella! That's my life right there – always getting everyone else ready to go to the ball, and never going myself."

If that's how you feel, you need to get your hands on my second book *Your Salon Team*. You'll love it … and Cinderella gets a mention in there.

12

Imagine if you had to continue to perform your role in that play forever. You'd go insane, right? You'd have to mix it up and change the characters or the setting. Maybe tweak the costumes or the lighting. You'd want to add some excitement to a tired, over-told story.

Do you see where I'm going with this?

Recommending retail in your salon is the same. You need to first learn your lines as they were written. Get the standard version down pat. Then, and only then, can you alter the message and mix it up a bit. The client might be hearing your story for the first time (or maybe the second time). It needs to be the exact same information with the exact same outcome, just told in a different way. This might be the hundredth (or even thousandth) time you've explained the benefits of double shampooing or placing the product in the right place. It's old information to you but it might be the first time anyone's bothered to explain it to this client. You can't change the ending, the "happy ever after" part, because that's the result, the outcome your client needs to solve their problem. What you can change is how you deliver the story.

You should have heard some of the ways I'd explain things! Lots of variation on a theme, I can tell you. Yet, still the exact same information. Why not get creative and pimp your product story?

Do you know your lines?

If your salon floor or beauty room is this stage and you are the performer on the stage, do you know your lines? Do you know what to say and when to say it? I still know my lines. I haven't worked in a salon for years yet could recite my product spiels in my sleep, standing on my head. You and your team need to be able to do the same.

If you're confident in your product knowledge (for *every* product you stock) and you know instantly what products suit each client, what their choices are, how much they should use and when, then I think you can answer *YES, I do know my lines.*

Now you just need to practise them.

I bet you've never practised what you'd say to someone if they said, "Nah, I don't want any".

Or what you'd say to someone who tells you flat out, "It's too expensive".

Or what you'd say to someone who says, "I just get mine from the supermarket, it's way cheaper".

If you haven't practised, you won't have the confidence of someone who's read their lines over and over and knows what they'll say in any given situation.

The first time you do something is almost always harder than the second time. Why? Because you take the learnings out of the first experience and you apply it to the second experience.

12

As you know, I love yoga. It challenges my fitness, my strength and my flexibility but it also "calms my farm" and by farm, I mean my head. Someone once said to me, "You clean your teeth every day and yet very few people make time to clean the mind".

That's what yoga does for me. It clears my mind.

But I had to work at it to see the improvements. Every time they ask you to stand on one leg and balance, I'm always much better when I do the other side, the other leg. I thought it was because I naturally start on the right-hand side but I tested it to see. It doesn't matter if I start with the left-hand side or the right-hand side, the first attempt is still not as good as the second attempt. Why? Because I've just practised and I've learnt something during that practice which I take through to my second attempt.

Retail is the same. When you absorb all the information about what the product does and what the benefits are it's easy to focus on the good results, the positive questions or comments your clients might have.

Most of you don't factor in the shitty questions, the ones that come firing from left field. The questions you hadn't imagined them asking. What happens? You get thrown off balance. Your confidence falters. In your head, you translate that to mean, "retail is not my thing". In reality, you just need to learn your lines, rehearse all possible conversations and go on stage fully prepared for anything that might come your way.

Why not get someone else on your team to ask you a couple of curve-ball questions around each of your products? Get them to complain that they don't want to be sold to while having their service done in your business. This eliminates the fear you have. If it ever happens, you're ready and *Boy, oh boy!* – watch your confidence grow.

In so many situations we're held back by not knowing what to say or how to deal with people's reactions. So you freeze and the rude, grumpy party wins. I'd hate that to be the case for you. When you know what to do, your confidence booms and your performance shines. People don't have to buy what you recommend; you just have to know that you've done the best job you possibly can of solving their problems.

Think about the first time you cut a wriggly kid's hair. It's a struggle between getting it cut quickly (because you know the longer it takes, the worse they get) and not darting too fast around his head that you take his eye out with your scissors. But you practise and practise and you get better at it.

It's a wonder we get as far as we do. Hairdressers are so resilient. Often we're not trained in a third of the things we're expected to do, yet for the most part, we're optimistic and happy campers. Real troopers. We just crack on with it and work shit out.

Try being a little more prepared and you'll be blown away with the confidence developing in you and your team.

I have a soft spot for hairdressers. It's my birds-of-a-feather-stick-together thing.

All the above applies to the beauty therapist, too. I just chose the kid's haircut for the drama of the pointy scissors. It's a stage, remember.

12

If you worked on a construction site, you'd put on your hat and your boots to protect your head and your feet. You'd wear a hi-vis shirt or vest. You wouldn't be allowed on site without all three. This is where we make a big mistake in hair and beauty settings. We recommend products to customers when we don't have the right gear to protect ourselves. By gear, I mean knowledge.

> **"You need to first learn your lines as they were written."**

We don't have the knowledge because we are under-rehearsed. And then we wonder why we don't perform well or get the results we expected.

To get the most out of practising, you need your team to be truthful about what product knowledge they already have. Then you can start training them, starting with quizzing them.

Next, you film your performance and have your team do the same for themselves. Everyone has a smartphone, so there's nothing to stop you or your team filming how you answer the various questions a client might ask.

Play it back and see how you can improve. You can do this over and over again without anyone else ever knowing about it. Or, if your team's fully on board, perhaps you can share your videos around and discuss them together. You can praise the bits that work well and help each other with the parts where you fumble. Practice makes perfect, guys!

Years ago, much to the horror of my team, I filmed them during role play consultations. It took some convincing to get them on board, but we got there.

The deal was that I would not share or show the videos to anyone else and I'd delete them completely at the end of the training. It was a fair deal so we got on with it. Once we got past the giggling, it was a rewarding exercise. My team discovered that they were skilled at recommending, that they came across as very professional.

Some were more confident than others but the beauty of having it on film was being able to stop at any point and have a discussion before re-starting the footage. We paused whenever the girls felt someone used a really cool word to describe something and we wrote it up on the salon mirror with a chalkboard pen. Across the group we collected several words we felt were powerful and empowering to both the stylist and the client.

Here are some of those chosen words (including sample sentences):

consistent: Your skin will improve if you're consistent with your cleansing.

extension: Looking after your tan will give you the extension you'll love.

ongoing: Replacing moisture in your hair is always going to be ongoing.

structure: A skin routine with a good structure means you'll be able to follow through.

replenish: With all the heat tools you use, you need to be mindful to replenish the moisture.

support: I'm here to support you, so you always look and feel your best.

Remember: it's a stage. Learn your lines, use the right words and your audience will be thrilled. The play is titled *The Salon Experience* and you have the lead role: the salon expert. You're all starring in the same role in your various salons, in every city and little town across the globe.

Your opening night is every time you approach a client to do the consultation. Think about slipping into your costume, putting on your face and then the curtain comes up. You're on!

Flicking the switch as you step on stage.

You need a trigger to set you off – a go switch. For me, I had this little leather apron.

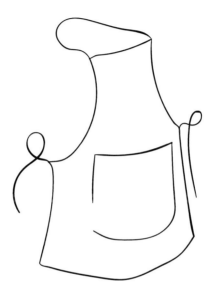

It's so soft. I've had it for years and still wear it at home when I'm baking. I had it custom-made in Bali. Something happens when I tie that apron on. It makes me step up. I become all polished and professional. It brings back many wonderful memories. If only it could talk! Actually, best it doesn't.

That apron was my trigger point. Once I tied those apron straps, I was stepping on stage. I had a job to do and I did it beautifully. Without that little black apron, it just didn't feel right. I could manage but it wasn't the same. It's the very same apron I'm wearing on the front cover of this book.

Maybe it's pinning on your nametag or applying fresh lipgloss just before you greet your client. Perhaps it's that last look in the mirror when you whisper to yourself: *You've got this!*

Identify a trigger that works for you, that sparks your transformation into your character – the salon expert. Then step on stage, brimming with confidence.

You might not have a hard hat and work boots to protect you, but you do have a healthy, confident emotional state to see you through your performance.

Kick-arse kick-starter.

Remember that product you scripted after reading Chapter 11? Re-script it. That's right, craft an alternative script including at least two of the powerful words listed above. Practise it, practise it, then step on stage and deliver your lines.

thirteen

chapter

13

The power of personal.

In today's world, we're outsourcing more things than ever to technology. We need to celebrate the fact that our industry can never be taken over by technology. We won't ever be replaced by a machine or a robot. Our people-to-people contact makes us unique.

It's a privilege to be a part of your clients' lives. They come and see you when they've got something special on – an upcoming occasion or a reason to celebrate and feel their best. They also come in when they're broken, sad, unhappy or just plain worn out and they're desperate to feel better about themselves, to be pampered and cared for. You see it all. That's what I loved the most. I used to say, "I'm a number cruncher. They come as a number 4 or a 5 and I send them out as a number 10." Being part of their lives was mostly a truckload of fun.

Hairdressing and beauty therapy differs from other careers because we physically touch our clients. We connect on a human level, not only through touching but also by being a person who cares. The strength of that emotional connection will always set you apart from your competitors. And it's all about trust.

Unlike product buying where you can easily compare one item to another, there are multiple things to consider when comparing services. For starters, there are the creative interpretation and the actual experience itself.

Products sales aren't like this. Your clients can readily compare buying a product from you to buying a product from a big budget warehouse store. The product itself is exactly the same when they get it home.

Salon owners often complain about the products they sell also being sold in big warehouses. It's difficult to compete on price – the big guys have incredible buying power. A salon can never beat them on that level.

What you can beat them on is knowledge. Can you honestly say you're doing your job and engaging your clients, explaining how to use the product? Every time? Every visit? Your world would change, if you did for only half your clients, half of the time. Because they're never going to get that product knowledge at a warehouse store. You need to stop the blame game. It's overdone and so yesterday. Just read on and discover more about the edge you have over your competition.

Most people wouldn't go out of their way to save a dollar or two. Most people are crazy busy. That's where you can help them. OK, I concede, some of your clients might choose the cheap option for their products. But are they your A grade clients? Or are you busy hanging about with the D grade clients? You know that D clients will drain the life out of you, one way or another. The only way to move up the scale away from D clients to the awesome A clients is to deliver a better service. To raise the bar.

The power of engagement.

If you think you're going to compete with the big warehouse stores you're wrong. You can't compete with them on price alone.

You could change your stock to a range that's never sold in David Jones, Myer or a mega store. That's your choice and it might well be the right choice for you. But it's not your biggest challenge. Your biggest challenge is that you don't engage your clients with exceptional customer service. You don't deliver the personal touch that sets you apart from those retail stores. And what about the online stores that offer huge discounts? They're always going to be there. Your edge is in your people-to-people connection, your ability to show exceptional attention to detail, premium care that your clients simply can't get online.

Try these things that your clients will never get from an online shopping experience:

- Flip the lid and let your client smell the product.
- Put a little product on the back of their hand and let them feel it.

- Let them feel the quality of the packaging and the all-round presentation.
- Offer them a sample.

I'm always popping into salons. I go up to the counter and ask questions about the products to see how much knowledge they have and how enthusiastic they are about helping me. I think maybe once, someone offered me a sample in a beauty salon. But I don't think anyone has ever offered me one in a hair salon. Why is that?

Many product companies avoid using samples. They think you should just be able to do your job and recommend the product. Yes, in theory that's true. And in theory kids should be able to make their own beds and school lunches by the time they're 10 years of age. That didn't happen in my house. Let's get real here: there's theory and there's reality.

Using samples to transform your retail sales.

When I decided to make some big changes with my team about how we were going to educate some 70 clients every week about buying products, I needed to get a great plan in place. I do love a plan!

The product company we used didn't make samples so I needed to get creative. Not far from my salon was a photo developing store. I asked a guy working there to save me the clear Fuji canisters from the rolls of 35mm film coming in for development. I didn't want the black Kodak ones; I wanted to be able to see through the container.

The team and I decided together that every single client would leave the salon with a sample of something: styling gel, wax, leave in conditioner … anything. As long as they left with a sample, we were on track to change every "doesn't" in our database to a "does".

> **Clients are *grateful for you showing interest in them*, finding out about their struggles and offering solutions. It works.**

One sample per visit. Every visit. We labelled each sample with permanent marker and added relevant notes to the computer. The only time we ever gave someone two samples was if they were taking a shampoo and conditioner pair.

We were very clear that we gave them enough for one use only. We didn't waste product and they knew exactly how much to use. In only a matter of months, our retail sales grew to an all-time high. Often the client would say, "Don't give me the sample, I'll just take it with me today, save me coming back. If you think I need it, then I need it."

We all had incredible learning around our little sample pots. We discovered that people wanted our opinion and that when we gave it, they very often acted on our advice and bought the recommended products.

It was that simple. I suggest starting with the sample because it's free. Many hairdresser and beauty therapists have blockages around the cost of the products they're recommending. While you might consider the sample method a little slow, if you're patient and consistent it works every time. Clients are grateful for you showing interest in them, finding out about their struggles and offering solutions. It works.

Today you can readily buy tiny containers for samples. Fish and chip shops put tartare sauce in them. Just check online and you'll readily source some to use in your salon.

Make a new system with your team around every client leaving with either a product or a sample of a product.

The "Nonna move".

I call this everyone leaves with a sample the "Nonna move". I was blessed with the best mother-in-law ever. I called her Mum when I married her son. She was just fabulous and her generosity was huge. You never left her house without something. Sometimes I just said YES to shut her up.

"Lisa you wanta parsley?"

"No thanks, Mum."

"You wanta lemons?"

"No thanks, Mum."

"You wanta some sauce? Hey what you want? You wanta something."

Heaven forbid if I left empty-handed.

That's why I call the sampling my "Nonna move".

You musta leave witha something.

Not everyone buys online.

I've never had much luck shopping online I always seem to get it wrong. I usually get a colour I didn't want, a size that isn't mine, or a delivery that takes forever and I end up having to chase them up. Maybe I'm the problem. I'm not very patient. I don't do enough research, I buy the first one and I don't read the fine print. It's pretty much lucky dip.

And I'd much prefer to speak with a person when I'm buying something. I like talking to people; it just seems to work better for me. I'm *that* person who asks for directions long before I'm lost. I ask ahead, just in case I'm going to get lost. Apparently that's not how online shopping works.

A woman living in my street is the exact opposite – she's mastered the art of online shopping. She's a hoarder in the real sense. I'm not exaggerating. She's very odd, hardly goes out at other than going to the post office and she's always having a parcel of some sort delivered. I'm sure she has a lot of online shopping successes. I also know she's had her share of disasters.

It doesn't seem to bother her; she simply ships them back. Just recently she showed me a handbag that she'd paid $12 for. She didn't realise the handbag was for a child about five years of age. She thought it was for an adult. She paid $8 on postage and couldn't be bothered sending it back. Too bad if the child was a smoker because the bag was so small, half a packet of cigarettes wouldn't have squeezed into it!

We're all different. That's what makes the world go around. We need to celebrate and accept that some of us shop online and some of us prefer the good old-fashioned service you can provide in your salon if you put your mind to it.

If you have retail stock in your hair and beauty business, forget about telling people the boring stories about people preferring to buy online. Just get on with your job. If you were to engage your clients effectively, those online sales wouldn't be there. Professionals who care for their clients get results. Nine out of ten of your clients would prefer to buy products from you ... if only you'd give them what they're really looking for.

Kick-arse kick-starter.

Get personal. Tomorrow, every time you use a product on a client, flip the lid and invite them to smell it. Just to see what happens.

fourteen

chapter

Give a guarantee (because you give a shit).

14

I don't get why many salons don't offer a money back guarantee on retail products. It's easy. *If you're not delighted with this product, then simply return it to us within 14 days and we'll replace it or give you your money back.*

I know. Most of you are worried you'll have these people bringing in three-quarter used shampoo bottles months later saying they only just bought it and don't like it.

It's not going to happen. Most of your clients are genuinely good people and those few dodgy ones have got better things to do than return a bottle of shampoo. Most of your clients are lucky if they get their kids to school on time every day. Buying products and then changing their minds is not high on anyone's list, trust me.

But I'll tell you what *is* going to happen.

The client standing in your salon will get a real sense that you care, that you "give a shit". They'll feel they can trust you. You'll instantly stand out from people who don't.

You need to check with your product supplier about offering the guarantee. If your staff are well-trained in the range you stock, there's a very big chance the company will support your guarantee. Not so much if it's obvious your team are relying on guesswork when they're recommending products.

14

> ❝ **Most of your clients are genuinely good people** and *those few dodgy ones have got better things to do than return a bottle of shampoo.* ❞

You could come up with a sentence about your commitment and add your product guarantee on all your marketing material. Certainly, use the guarantee when you're with a client and they're deciding whether or not to take a product home with them.

A solid guarantee eliminates the client's fear of risk. It helps them tick off the *What have I got to lose?* question on their before-I-buy check-list.

Marketing giants swear by offering the peace of mind of a guarantee. It's all part of direct response marketing where the aim is to get people to respond now, or purchase on impulse. The money back guarantee is designed to take away any lingering doubt and get the sale across the line. Unlike these big players, I want you to care about whether or not the product you recommend is the right fit. Your professional expertise and product knowledge tell you it is, but you're human. And so is your client. You care enough to want your client fairly compensated for the expense in the rare instances where the product isn't right for them. It's a whole different ballgame to the one the big guys play. I'm fairly sure most of them have no care factor. They just move huge volumes of product and cost in a certain number of returns into their pricing models.

14

My sister Pauline gets to the shops about six times a year if she's lucky. She lives on a farm and her workload's the same every day of the week. When she does manage a shopping day, she often buys things in a hurry. She's your "give me that in two other colours please" style of shopper.

I only recently discovered she even buys things from those dodgy over-hyped TV sales channels. She'd been housebound due to an injury and happened to tune in to daytime TV. She confessed she'd bought one of those gizmos you stand on and balance while it wobbles you. It's supposed to shake all your fat off.

I said, "I can't believe you bought that! What were you thinking?"

"I thought I could stand on it while I did the ironing at night," she said.

"And did you?"

"No. One of the kids showed up and thought it was fabulous. I haven't seen it since."

"I could have told you that," I said. "You tend to lose most things to one of your kids." And we had a great laugh about it all.

14

She added that she'd only bought it because of the money back guarantee. She thought it must have lived up to the claims if the seller was prepared to offer a guarantee.

Exactly my point – in my sister's mind, the guarantee eliminated the risk.

Yet, she can't return it. "I'm not getting the results I wanted," she said. "But that's not the company's fault. I'm not using it, so I can't possibly get the results."

A money back guarantee will take the risk away and the number of people who take you up on the return of a product is very small, especially when you're making sound recommendations. The guarantee simply demonstrates to your client that it matters to you that you get it right for them. And, if not, they come back to you and give you the opportunity to recommend another solution to their problem. Win, win.

Kick-arse kick-starter.

Phone your product rep today and ask them to
back you in offering your clients a money back
guarantee on their products. What have you got
to lose?

14

fifteen

chapter

Four things to try in your salon right now.

15

Number #1 try-it-now.
Focus on the client's *real* problem.

They know they have problems but most don't realise they have underlying problems.

To get to the real (or underlying) problem, you need to find out more. You do that by asking better questions. Clients often don't know what they don't know. Before you can give them a lasting solution, you'll need to identify what they do know and what they don't know … then close the gap.

You might have to scratch around like a farmyard chook – over here, over there and back over here a little bit. One scratch doesn't usually unearth what you're looking for.

If you've ever had the pleasure of sitting and watching chooks when they're let out of their cage, you'll get what I mean. They're so busy scratching and looking around, scratching and looking and scratching again until they find what they're looking for. One scratch or one question won't get you the result you need.

It's the same when we're in the salon looking after clients – one scratch is never enough. If you have clients who don't accept your retail advice and take products home with them, then you need to scratch around a little more.

15

People take Panadol all the time, right? They don't take it because they have a paracetamol deficiency. No, that's silly. They take it to mask another problem.

Clients often tie their hair up. Why, because they can't manage it when it's out. Why? Because it's dry. Why is it dry? Because it's in terrible condition. Can you fix that with a product? Of course you can!

Some people wear foundation like it's icing on a cake. Why? Because they don't like their natural skin. Why? They have pimples and blemishes. Why? Because they're not aware of a better skincare plan. Why? Because they haven't had the right therapists scratching around for better solutions. Can you solve this with a product? You bet you can!

15

Most people don't realise you can fix most of their problems with product. And there are many of you standing behind your salon chair or treatment bed who haven't worked it out either.

Think about it.

It's the "too much" story

Too thin, too heavy, too oily, too nothing, too fly-away, too frizzy. And in skin it's: too oily, too dry, too many breakouts, too many sunspots, too many lines. Most things can be fixed with the right product.

This is how I want you to start every conversation with your client from this day on.

"If I could solve your biggest problem today what would that be?"

That one question will start you on a journey of scratching around like a farmyard chook. Never forget you need more than one scratch to find a worm.

Number #2 try-it-now.
Explain the moisture triangle to your clients.

If you're serious about the results your clients are getting, you need to make it easier for them to understand.

There are three fundamental things you need to check on when it comes to moisture for both hair care and skincare.

Let's start with hair.

Step 1: Check what your client uses when they wash their hair. Is it quality **shampoo and conditioner**?

Step 2: What about **leave-in treatments**? Do they use a heat protector or leave-in moisturiser? Are they using it every wash? Is it the right one for their hair?

Step 3: Do they have a **salon strength treatment**? There are many choices, from the spa types that come with massages and hot towels, to the Plex group types and the smoothing keratin type ones. These are game-changers and you need to educate your clients around these exciting options I call the "big guns of hair".

Finally, explain to your client that if they want amazing hair like they see in magazines, they need to do all three points of the triangle, and frequently. Unless you're offering all three, you aren't giving your clients what they need. And you won't ever get optimum results.

I'm a bit over explaining this to random people I meet who admire my curls and then go on to tell me their hair is curly and they can't manage it so they tie it up. They haven't had the right information. Curls need to be in top condition or you have a frizzy mess. I tell them to put their hand in their pocket and invest in all three corners of the moisture triangle.

I've even drawn it on a serviette in a café and told a girl to go back to their so-called "fabulous hairdresser" and tell her this is what you need (all the while I'm thinking, imagine how fabulous she will be when she gets the moisture right.)

Now, let's look at beauty clients.

Step 1: The daily **cleanser and moisturiser** is the first place you check. Are they using the best products for their skin?

Step 2: Next is the "alphabet" test. All those lovely **vitamins and the serums** on the market. The special formulas that prep your skin for the next level of care. And, of course, **eye creams and skin exfoliates**, too.

Step 3: Then it's the **in-salon treatments** – anything from microdermabrasion's, Laser LED to Fraxel, skin needling and all of the amazing peels. Once again, the big guns.

15

The moisture triangle is what everyone needs if they're serious about the results. Your clients are simply missing out if they don't understand their options. It's your job to know your stuff and to share that knowledge with them.

Number #3 try-it-now.
Buy what you sell.

It's disappointing that salon staff often haven't experienced the services or used the products they recommend. How the hell can you recommend something you haven't experienced first-hand?

I once worked with a skincare clinic where the girls had never had the needling. Guess what? No one was recommending it either. There's your problem, right there. We had a big chat and discovered it was down to equal parts time challenge and equal parts care factor (or lack of). I took that to mean they didn't care enough to make the time.

We made it mandatory that every team member was to experience every treatment – in business hours and at no cost to them. In return, they'd recommend the services like there was no tomorrow. We lost one team member who decided during the process that it wasn't the right place for her and moved on. Fair enough. The rest of the team blossomed like you wouldn't believe. From then on, every time I visited the clinic, someone had a red peeling face or eyebrows recovering from a tattoo. It was the best thing we ever did. The girls were living proof that the treatments worked – walking examples of before, during and after.

15

Experiencing every service and every product they sold was a game-changer. They went from selling no after-laser balm to having every client using it. The results for the clients and the business were 100-fold better because of it.

Number #4 try-it-now.
Ignore the negative chatter in your head about price.

One of the biggest blocks we have around selling products to clients is the price. Because we source products at cost, we see full price as expensive. We also judge people on what they say, what they wear and whether we think they have the money to spend. Instead, we should just get on with doing our jobs.

15

You'd be surprised who has money to spend. Often it's not who you think.

I remember doing a training night in a big team of both hair and beauty girls. These girls had a serious problem with rounding the price down. *Just make it $40* type of thing, when it was meant to be $46. In small communities it can be even more challenging to charge full price; everyone's a friend or relative.

We worked hard together on this mindset and thankfully stopped the behaviour. My next challenge was to introduce a solid system for retail. A one in, all in pact. Together, we came up with one and all agreed to follow it no matter what came our way. It was designed to eliminate the "I don't think she will buy a product" chatter in the team members' heads. My aim was for them to treat every client equally. In other words, just do their job without the judgement. I asked them to stick to the system we agreed to and put in place that night.

They all said they'd do it "my way" (which was really "our way") for one week and report back. I agreed that was fair and left the meeting.

The next morning Marie the salon owner looked at her first booking and thought, "Shit! It's Betty."

Betty was this little old nanna who had a chin wax and an eyebrow wax. Nothing more. Nothing less. She had the exact same treatment every fourth Wednesday at 9am. Betty was like clockwork.

Marie thought, "A deal's a deal, and I'm doing this. Every client, every time. I will do as I said I'd do."

Marie took three products into the beauty room. That was the deal, to think ahead and make suggestions around solving problems.

Marie was certain Betty would only have her two usual areas waxed. She was going to be a tough one. You know those nanna purses with the clasp in the middle? Betty always had the correct money folded on the right-hand side of her nanna purse.

Marie did the wax and said, "If you like, Betty, I can give you a little express make over and cover up your redness from the wax. It'll only take me five minutes. Do you have the time to spare?"

So, she did a foundation powder, a blush and a mascara.

Marie took the hand-held mirror and showed Betty.

Betty thanked Marie and added, "I'd all but given up on making myself pretty. I haven't worked for years now and I'm so out of touch. I don't know where to start anymore. What you did looks fresh and not like I'm wearing makeup. You're so clever, Marie. Do you think I could do it myself?"

" *My aim was for them to treat every client equally.* "

"Absolutely and if you have trouble just come in and any of the girls will give you a lesson."

"That was very thoughtful of you, Marie, to take the time with me. How much are they?"

Marie left the room to find out and by memory it came to about $175. Betty said, "Yes, that's fine Marie, as long as they're good quality."

Marie assured her they were. Betty flicked the other side of her nanna purse open and there was a wad of rolled up fifties (or pineapples, as I like to call them).

Marie could not get to the phone quick enough to tell me what had happened.

You see, Marie had been judging Betty mostly because she always had the money ready. That just wasn't fair. Marie and her team followed the new system. At times they got off track, but for the most part they just did their job and did it without that negative chatter in their head. So much nicer for everyone.

Sure, the Betty thing could have gone either way. She could easily have said, "I'm fine. Thanks anyway." And if that's the worst that happens, I reckon we can all cope just fine.

15

Kick-arse kick-starter.

Tomorrow, ask every client you look after, "If I could solve your biggest problem today, what would that be?" Stand back, listen and watch the conversations unfold.

sixteen

chapter

16

Float like a butterfly, sting like a bee.

What's the magic ingredient you need to become the black belt retail person in your salon?

Let me tell you.

It's confidence. The thing that will change the way you do everything in life will also drive your success in salon retail.

As animals, we're all drawn to the more confident ones in our species. If you watch any David Attenborough show, you'll see it's everywhere. When animals are fighting for survival. When they're finding a mate. Confidence is this thing inside us, an intangible that can help us command respect and rise above the average.

Muhammad Ali said it beautifully: *I am the greatest. Watch me as I float like a butterfly and sting like a bee.* It's hard to say that sentence without smiling.

Mick Jagger is a sliver of a man, yet he's strutted around on stage for more than forty years. Then there are Madonna, Tina Turner and Tom Jones. They all command respect and ooze off-the-scale confidence.

Yet none of them are, in a purely physical sense, beautiful. The combination of experience and knowledge they have in their chosen field gives them an edge. That edge is confidence. Their confidence makes them stand out.

I went with my 25-year-old daughter to see Tom Jones last year. It was her idea – she knew I'd taken myself off to see Tom Jones when I was pregnant with her and thought it would be fun to go together again. It was a relatively small venue and we managed to wiggle our way right to the front. What Tess couldn't get over was his confidence. She said, "Mum, there's something about that man." It wasn't until we were halfway home in the car that she said, "It's his confidence that's so appealing. He just oozes confidence."

16

These people are as they are because they know their stuff – inside-out and upside-down. Have they always been this way? Probably not. They must have started somewhere, right?

Yes, just like you in your salon business, they started somewhere.

The big question for you is: How do I build my confidence? First things first. You need to get together a plan of action. This plan is going to be around your product knowledge, because nothing builds confidence like knowledge. Let's get planning.

Count every product you sell.

Now you need to divide that number by the number of products you can learn about in a week. Three? Six? Nine? The number you set yourself will depend on how serious you are about getting to learn the moves "like Mick Jagger".

Knowledge on every product you stock will bring you unbelievable confidence.

Take the time to role-play and as you do, use only the products you sell. Go to www.zingretailresources.com.au and download our PDF specially created so you can fill in all your product details and have them all together. I want you to fill in the answers to all the questions in that download.

I suggest you learn three products starting on a Monday, another three on Wednesday and another three on Friday. Then get tested on all nine and start over. If you make a mistake on any of those nine, keep learning them for another week. Then repeat the process until you get to the end. Every product. Everything you need to know.

The trick is to learn them by saying the key info out loud and repeating it, over and over again.

You need to know not only who the product is best suited to, but also how much your client should be using, how often they should use it, the size options it comes in and the cost. Once you know these things about every product retailed in your salon, you've earned the right to strut around like Mick Jagger. Or you might take Mohammed's approach and be floating around the salon like a butterfly – when you hear a problem you can solve, you sting like a bee with your knowledge.

Most people remain unfocused and full of reasons why they don't finish what they set out to do. The truth is, most fill in the first one or two pages of the product form, learn those few and then life gets in the way.

Your commitment is the key, your stick-ability. It's not that much of an effort once you get started. The products aren't that complicated. Many have similarities, common ingredients and benefits that you can group together in your head. Generally, there are around four price variances and maybe four size options. Most have one key ingredient, not twenty-seven. Just knuckle-down and get on with learning them. It's not that hard.

16

Focus on your end goal. Imagine how confident you'll be once you know every product inside and out. People don't fail and then give up. It's the other way around: they give up first and then they fail.

A few years back, when my daughter was studying medicine, we had drawings of body parts on the back of the toilet door and all around the house. The names she was learning to pronounce and spell were much more challenging than Keratin or seaweed extract. They were words like sphenopalatine ganglioneuralgia and onychocryptosis. And these were the easy ones!

You need to get on with your plan of being the salon with the best reputation in town for product knowledge and all round confidence. Wouldn't you love to hear people saying that your salon team really know their stuff? You can't buy that sort of publicity. It's an amazing buzz to have a new client arrive at your salon and say, "My friend told me to come here and ask about my frizzy hair. She said you'd know for sure what to do, that you're all fabulous here."

> **"** *People don't fail and then give up. It's the other way around:* ***they give up first and then they fail.* "**

16

Buddy-up to boost your learning.

Learning is always more successful if you join forces. I suggest you get a buddy. You can work together to test each other and stay on track.

Now that you've compiled your salon's entire product list, you know exactly what you need to get through. Decide how many you can reasonably learn in a week. Maybe it's 9, as I suggested above. Let's say you stock 44 products, divide that by 9 and you'll be on top of them all in less than 5 weeks. You might even decide you already know half the products inside out. Once you take those out of the equation, you only need to divide 22 by 9 to see you can get your learning done in under

3 weeks. When you really hone in and break it down, your mission is more than do-able.

Stick to your plan.

Now you have the plan. All you need do is to stick to it! And get your team to stick to it. Maybe arrange a surprise gift for the person who's most focused. Public recognition shows you're serious and helps develop good habits going forward. Don't be shy about asking your product company to help you out with a prize or two.

You can also make sure your clients are getting the same consistent retail care and that your team are doing their job of recommending by choosing a hero product. A hero product is your standout product. It's something every client should be using. It might be a sunscreen, a cleanser or, in hair, a heat protector. You can get really creative and proactive when you're profiling a hero product. You can showcase it in your newsletter alongside testimonials of people who can't live without it. You can display the product in your salon window with props. If the packaging is blue, you might put other blue things with it like flowers or a stunning pair of killer heels in blue. Think about something that gets people talking and grabs their attention. You might have a special offer around it – not a discount, more like a gift with purchase.

The timing will vary according to the cycle of your clientele. As an example, this product could be the hero in your salon for two months, meaning you only get six heroes each year to play with.

16

Aim for your clients to always feel there's something fresh going on. When they walk into your salon or clinic, they should get a sense of newness, that stuff's going on, that you're not stuck in the same old, same old. Most of all, they should get a huge sense of confidence from each and every one on your team about not only the hero product, but every product in your salon.

Kick-arse kick-starter.

Right now, spend five minutes in front of your product shelf choosing your salon's first hero product. Next spend 10 minutes jotting down some notes about how you and your team can promote and recommend this product. Now you have the makings of a plan.

16

seventeen

chapter

17

One in, all in (getting your team on board).

Loyalty love starts at home. Your salon team must be loyal to whatever products you put on your salon's shelf. Check what your team members are using on themselves and you'll probably find it's not the case.

17

If you're serious about the results you get with your retail sales, you need to be generous with the products you send your team home with.

Think about this. If you go into a clothing store, say Kookai, the sales assistants are not wearing anything but Kookai, right? You never go into Zara and catch them wearing Kookai or vice versa. They sign-off on the dress rules at the beginning of their employment and they stick to it.

Remember back in Chapter 8 I wrote about the team member being open for ideas at the beginning (a martini glass rather than a champagne glass)? Fashion retailers choose team members who can wear their brand and wear it well. It's no different for us in the hair and beauty sector. We need to find the right fit. The difference is that too often we're searching for the right "look". What you need to find is the right "mind".

> **" Those who start off with half a plan *tend to get* half a result. "**

It's disappointing when your salon team members aren't interested in exploring the use of your entire product range. They not only get stuck on one or two pet products for their clients, they also do the same for themselves. Laziness and/or money are often the cause. They won't pay for the products and they choose to spend their money elsewhere. When you (and your team members) don't use the salon products yourself, you're sending an underlying message to your client. Hairdressers and beauty therapists won't recommend products they don't believe in. The challenge is that often they don't educate themselves beyond the basics; they think they know more than they do. Their ability to solve a problem is narrow and their retail knowledge matches – basic at best.

The real deal matters.

How do you get your team to change their small thinking? The simple answer is: talk to them. You must get them to understand your point of view, that being the "real deal" matters to you, and to your clients. And it should matter to your team, too.

I believe you should offer your team members a hefty cut on purchase price of products. Fashion retailers do this for their staff because it works as an added incentive. Find a staff discount point that you think is fair and pass it on to them. Every team member, every product they purchase. Be generous. I gave my team 40% off the RRP. They were always happy with that. Consider adding another level in here. Maybe something like this: if a team member reaches a consistent (agreed) level of retail, they could have a "retail buddy" and you extend the 40% deal to their best friend or mother, to sweeten the offer and give them incentive to grow.

17

All for one, one for all.

It's rare for team members to outshine the business owner. It's safe to say that salon teams are only ever as good as the salon leader. If you want lasting change when it comes to retail in your salon business, then you need to take it on as a team, not as a collection of individuals doing their best on different days. You must introduce and execute the changes as a team. Otherwise you'll get initial results but they'll be short-lived.

To make the shift you need it must be "one in, all in". No exceptions.

If you, the salon owner, know "how to" and consistently recommend retail, that's great news. If you're not good at retail yourself, it's bad news. You're the team leader. Whether you like it or not, they look to you for direction.

Often salons consist of small teams of three or four where the team looks up to people doing the exact same job they are (with the added challenge of running the business). The rule of thumb is this: whoever is asking a team member (or members) to recommend retail needs to lead by example. The bonus for team members is knowing the direction is coming from someone who has walked (and is walking) in their shoes. You understand their struggles, how hard it is to be consistent. You're not preaching from above, you're working side-by-side, in the next chair or beauty room. You're saying to your team, "Look, this can be done, we can recommend retail and it's important."

17

The corporate world is a different beast. Here, they often bring management in from elsewhere. From another department, another state, another sector. Sometimes, from another country. There is no personal connection between the leader and the team. They might have the luxury of a big team, but small salon teams have the advantage of knowing and connecting to one another.

Of course, problems do arise in our small teams. Often the scenario involves a team member being promoted to the management team. Often the management team is a team of one. It can be a lonely place when you're implementing team-wide change such as retail systems. Your colleagues are also your friends and often they're your family. It's challenging to enforce a system around product sales (or any system, really) in a friendly, social setting. Emotions can get in the way and cloud the truth. Expectations can differ.

The only way to address the issue effectively is for everyone to understand that you wear different hats at work and after work. Transition takes time, but you'll get there.

Everyone (including you) on the same page.

Start with a strong, confident plan of attack. Those who start off with half a plan tend to get half a result. Prepare for the worst and hope for the best. The corporate world would call this "risk management". I call it the "how could we stuff this up?" plan.

You need to document your plan because paper makes things official. It's proof of what was said and decided so you know you're all on the same page. (See Chapter 10 for more tips on planning.)

17

```
┌─────────────────────────┐     ┌─────────────────────────┐
│                         │     │                         │
│        RISK             │     │    STUFF THAT CAN        │
│     MANAGEMENT          │     │    GO TO TITS            │
│                         │     │                         │
└─────────────────────────┘     └─────────────────────────┘
```

Don't for a minute think your new retail system does not apply to you, just because you're the leader, the one asking the team to step-up. You need to get out of your high heels and step into your boots, your work boots. Get out of your comfort zone and into whatever place you're asking your team to go. You need to be transparent and tell them what you struggle with when it comes to recommending retail. Don't make excuses about how busy you are. If you don't get with the program, neither will they. Be honest. Open up about your wins (big and small) and your battles. Encourage them to do the same. Laugh together, support one another and just keep sticking to the plan.

Kick-arse kick-starter.

17

Do a quick informal survey of your team to find out what products they're using and why. Ask if you offering them a discount on the products you stock would change what they buy. You know what to do next.

eighteen

chapter

18

Your product rep is on your team, too.

In the movie *Erin Brokovitch*, Erin's boss asks her, "How did you do that?"

She turns to him and says, "Boobs, Ed. They're called Boobs." Well, in our industry, it's not boobs, it's your relationship with your product company that gets the job done. When it comes to effectively training your entire team in retail, what you need is a healthy relationship with your product rep. Get a great one on your team and it's as good as a having an amazing rack (or boobs, as Erin called them).

18

Direct access to your product company through your representative is gold. Never settle for an average rep. The right one will take you and your team to a whole new level. The good ones care about you and your salon business. Beware: if your product company sees you as a C or D grade account now, you have your work cut out for you. It can be done, but you need to start over and eliminate what I call "D grade" thinking and behaviour.

D and some C grade salons don't pay their accounts on time. The rep always has to chase them to get payment. C and D grade salons don't stock either the whole range or enough stock, so they run out of stock. All the time. They put off ordering because they have inconsistent cash in their business. When they do place an order, they want it filled yesterday. They have no system for ordering, so they phone in the stock order while the salon is noisy – one of the easiest ways to stuff up an order. When their order arrives wrong, they blame the rep.

The rep is so pleased to get the order he (or she) never bothers to explain that this is a shitty method of ordering.

C and D grade salons stock products they never use. From time-to-time they even try to get the rep to take the product back and swap it out, as if it's his (or her) fault the company made a product they can't sell. Truth is, there's nothing wrong with the product. Two streets away, in another salon, the very same product is so loved it flies off the shelf. The team love it, use it and recommend it.

C and D grade salons make excuses and blame everyone and everything else for their shortcomings.

C and D grade salons don't educate themselves. They don't go to industry education events so they stay in the same place and nothing changes.

When a salon owner bitches to me about a product company, I ask one question, "Are you closer to an A or a D grade salon?" They always tell me, "An A, for sure." Then I scratch around and find they're almost always nowhere near an A. And there's always a raft of reasons why.

The product rep (let's call him a he) doesn't confront you with your ordering shortcomings because to them, an order is an order. It all helps him hit his target and meet his budget. Ideally, he'd take the time to explain how he'd prefer to work with you. But he just sucks it up and nothing ever changes. And like you, he bitches to me about it.

I can see faults on both sides. Some product companies' reps are so weighed down with salon whingers, it's no wonder they often move on to selling something else

And there are too many salon owners who think running a salon team is your cross to bear. You bitch and moan about the team of dopes you have to work with. In truth, you get the team you deserve. Your team reflects what you think – you get what you think.

When I ask most salon owners if they think I'd tolerate that sort of behaviour if it were my salon, they answer emphatically, "No way!" So my question back is always, "So, why do you?"

18

Mostly it's because you don't have the tools yet to fight your way to a better place. I suggest reading my *Your Salon Team* book. It's full of tips on growing an awesome team. Your company rep is also on your team.

First things, first – you must develop an open and honest relationship with your rep around growing your retail business. The product company will train your whole team if they know you're serious about making long-term changes.

Everyone wins when your salon is kicking arse in retail.

Your clients will get their needs met and their problems solved, your team will be reaching their targets and your rep will be filling healthy, regular stock orders for you.

Your product company representative could well be the most under-used asset in our industry. It's no coincidence that great salons show respect to their reps. They are thoughtful about their time and the business respect is mutual. Those that are struggling are probably lucky to even get a visit from a rep.

Let me tell you about my own experience with product company reps. When I first opened my salon, I didn't pay much attention to retail. That's actually an understatement. I didn't know any better. The salon I worked in for 16 years didn't place real value on retail sales. He considered retail a nuisance, something you had to have. He had three salons and I know the one I worked in had the best product company account. Back then, we had no scales to measure products – it was "half of 6 and half of 7". I imagine we over-mixed and wasted an enormous amount of product.

The rep who looked after my boss's account always left me feeling it was a bit of a boys' club. They were always wheeling and dealing. I can remember putting away stock that we hadn't ordered; it was as though it fell off the back of a truck. I asked my boss about the rep. He said he was like a rat with a gold tooth. "Agh, forgetaboutit," he said in a strong Italian accent.

18

That seemed pretty much the norm back in the 80s. Today there are far better ways to keep track of stock.

When I left to open my own salon, I just continued using the brand that my boss was using and the rat with the gold tooth gave me the same discount as my boss and that was all there was to it.

It wasn't until Rob Seeley, the state manager from PPS, dropped in a bag of products to me personally that I gave any thought to changing product brands.

I loved the PPS products and hence my relationship with Rob and PPS started. I'd had my salon doors open for a few months by then and hadn't seen or heard of the product company I was with so my decision to change was an easy one.

Rob sent me along a few different reps but they all seemed as bad as one other, all cut from that same below-average cloth. My first decent product rep was Michelle Carra. I'd had a couple before her that didn't hang around that long. That's one of the frustrations with product companies. Many don't seem to be able to find good people. Well you know what I'm going to say about that, don't you? Product companies, you need to look inward and ask yourself this: *Are we the company of choice? Is this an awesome company to be working with? Does our company have a vision? Are we going places?*

In contrast, there are some great product companies out there who have no trouble attracting and keeping great staff. Just saying.

18

Product repping seems to be a very mobile career. Sometimes the long-time players leave and then pop up elsewhere and some even pop right back to where they started. It's like the game peek-a-boo you play with a baby in a pram. It's a small industry and you tend to come across the same faces popping in and out, playing peek-a-boo with you.

When your rep does do a disappearing act, you usually get a letter (in the mail) assuring you nothing has changed and that the part of Susie the rep will be now played by Sally the rep. It's a bit like the voice-over in the TV soap *Days of Our Lives*. "Victor is now being played by James O'Conner." And you're meant to just accept the new face and the old ways and not even notice the change. It's so impersonal. I wish product companies would understand the value in calling you, the salon owner, to explain the change and chat about how it will work. Make it personal. Pick up the phone, people.

Anyway, back to my new rep, Michelle. I didn't know my rep was being replaced until I got the standard delete-old-rep-insert-new-rep letter. When I read her name, it sounded familiar and sure enough, it turned out Michelle went to school with one of my sisters.

What a joy it was to have Michelle. She was a ripper, an absolute breath of fresh air. Michelle was the full bottle: she'd come to the salon at the right time on the right day and take to my product shelf. She was full of energy and excitement, telling me about the best of the monthly deals according to my ordering habits and placing my order correctly every single

18

time. She didn't hang around bitching and wasting my time. She might have a quick coffee but it was always work and I knew she respected my time. She'd be back in four weeks' time to do it all again, on time on cue. She was a machine. She trained my team up in product knowledge and gave them all a free product to try. Nothing was too much trouble.

And then she was gone. Just like that.

You know how I tell you that everyone is leaving? It's true, even your product reps are leaving. Michelle was moving up north to follow the sun and start afresh. I got the standard delete-Michele-insert-X letter. My next rep seemed like a nice enough chap, well-dressed with a happy disposition. Until he said he'd be back on a particular day, at a certain time and turned up three hours late. We didn't get off to a great start. Four weeks rolled around and this time he was a complete no-show. When I called to see if he'd forgotten me he said, "Sorry, something's come up this week."

I cracked it, phoned the state manager and said, "If you send him one more time, you can close my account. He's useless."

18

Turns out his excuse for lack of focus was he was dating a redheaded politician at the time and it was all-consuming. Like that has anything to do with my stock order. Years later he ended up living in The Lodge in Canberra with the red head and becoming Australia's first bloke.

Kick-arse kick-starter.

Think back over your dealings with your product rep during the last 6 months. What grading do you think your rep would give you as a client? Closer to an A or a D? Jot down the reasons why. Now you know where to start.

18

nineteen

chapter

19

Learning to love your product company relationship.

Product company reps are a mixed bag. Often they're worn down by exhausted salon owners. How hard would it be to keep your energy up when you're in and out of salons every day, and in every one of them you're hearing a broken record about how tough it is to run a salon?

You need to stop whinging to your product rep. They are not to blame for your woes. Instead, focus on building a positive, solid relationship with your rep to support the growth and success of your salon retail.

If you happen to have a great rep already, I salute you. I salute both. If your rep truly cares about you and your salon, hang on to him (or her) with all your might. Surprise them with gifts for their birthday and Christmas. Pen a thoughtful thank you

19

card and make sure they feel your appreciation. You'll not only stand out among the whingers, you'll be fostering a mutually advantageous relationship.

In contrast, if your product rep relationship is rocky, maybe you should be looking at your approach. For example, stop banging on about how hard it is to get free stuff these days. You know what I'm talking about: "I've spent $50K with you this year, I'm owed free products galore."

It's crap and you need to do away with that thinking all together. You'd be better spending your time becoming a better client to your product company. Put your energy into growing your retail spend and then you'll be winning on all sides.

Your product rep is a person doing their job, just like you and me. You need to get over your "what's in it for me?" thinking. I suggest you start by walking into a salon or three and seeing how you get treated. It's a sad truth that most salon staff are rude to most product reps. They treat them like they're God-botherers. No one should be treating anyone that way. Not ever. Not even if you're a slick, high-end city salon. I'd rather phone 100 country salons with an invitation to a presentation than one city salon – for the most part, you city salon owners are rude on the phone to me, too.

Sure, you get inundated with people wanting to speak with you, but kindness costs nothing. Take a minute or two, always be polite, and simply explain that you're happy to have a look later, if they just leave you the information.

If you know the brand and you know it's not your thing and won't ever be your thing, then make it clear you're not interested. Tell them you'd prefer they didn't call you away from your clients and that they can leave the information on the front desk. That's it.

Don't say you'll look at it if you have no intention of doing so. You're giving them false hope. Just be honest. Some companies have great education (all the good ones do). These special events are a great window into a company's culture and it's OK to go to an event even if you don't stock their brand.

I value education more than anything and going to an event or three is a good way to see how the company interacts with their clients, other salons just like you.

Does the education and service look like an improvement on what you're getting now with your existing brand, the one you currently stock? It's a great way to compare. It's the ultimate try before you buy.

The more events you attend, the better, right? Google, Gather and Go – remember that?

I've worked with some of the kindest, most thoughtful people. Yet, when I'm chatting with company reps, they tell me the very same people have been unwelcoming and rude to them. I say, "Are you sure? She couldn't possibly be rude."

"Well, she must have two heads," the rep tells me. "I can't even get a smile."

19

It's another symptom of our industry being riddled with "false nice".

NICE stands for: *Nothing Inside Cares Enough*. You keep getting annoying calls and people dropping in, where if you just cared enough to take the time to tell them the truth, you'd be doing everyone a favour. Most of all, your own reputation.

Try this, in your most genuine voice:

Just so you know, I am not interested in other products at this stage. I'm very happy with the range I have. If I can be really honest with you, I'm just not interested in anything else. I promise if I need something I will call you.

Then pause. Give them a chance to say a few words in return and if they bang on, then you might need to repeat part of the sentence.

It's not personal, it's business.

You don't make it clear what you want, so you go on wasting your time, and theirs. There's no need. Just deal with it honestly and openly. Be upfront.

I've often thought a sticker equivalent to the No Junk Mail might be the answer. What would it say? Maybe: *Not looking to change product companies anytime soon, so no need to drop in. Thank you.*

The risk, of course, is that you end up being more distanced from your community … and you're already isolated enough.

> ## " *NICE stands for:* *Nothing Inside* *Cares Enough.* "

My best tip is to sort them out, one-by-one. Make a list of those who calls on you and set aside a few minutes to have a look, ask a question or two about education, get some information. Do your part and make time to have a look. After you've had a look, either book in an education event with them and find out more or, if you know it's not for you, explain politely that it's not. Thank you, but no thank you.

OR you can have them drop off a brochure every month only for you to throw it in the bin? Really?

Do it or don't do it, I say. Make one decision, take action and move on. A reminder here: we all have just 24 hours a day.

There are some reps out there who are like those annoying blow-up clowns, the ones you punch in the face and they bounce straight back up at you. We've all met them, right? They hang about your salon hoping you'll find five minutes for them. And when you do manage to make the time, they misinterpret your politeness for interest in their offer and it seems doubly hard to loosen yourself from their clutches.

I'm grateful there aren't too many like this, but there are still a few around who remind me of the locals selling watches on Bali beaches. People have horror stories about being followed

19

for blocks. I've been to Bali far too many times. They don't follow me. I don't look and I don't speak. They soon learn I'm not biting. My sister, on the other hand, tends to show a tiny bit of interest and it's on. I must double-back and pull her away by the arm to save her, both of us laughing at the whole scenario. Most reps are not like that and they'll respond well to your honesty. Then you can both get on with the job of being awesome in your own way. Just remember: what you stock is your choice; it's your right as salon owner to choose what floats your boat.

Just show each other respect – after all, we are (or at least, should be) on the same team here.

You get nothing for nothing.

In the product companies' defence there are some salon owners who think they should get free things. What is that about? Why should you get free stuff from the company?

Nothing is ever free. There are always strings of some sort attached. There is no such thing as a free lunch. It's like credit card points – they get you on the hefty interest rates, then give you a gift to sweeten the deal and keep you from figuring it out. Any financial adviser will tell you to pay the card balance out every month. Most of you aim for that and most of you miss it. The game continues. The gift sweetens up the sour taste of paying the high interest rate on the balance you don't repay. No free lunch.

If your product rep is offering you extra things, it's in relation to a special deal. It might be a Buy 12 of these and we'll give you 2 for free deal. That's great if you need 12 of them. If not, don't get sucked in by the sweetener. Just buy what you need, nothing more, nothing less. Stick to your budget. What? You don't have a budget? How do you work out what you need?

A budget can be worked out for you. It will depend on your business model and once it's shown to you, you'll be amazed how clear and logical it is. This is one of the things salon owners really love us at ZING setting up for them. It eliminates the guesswork, stops all that head scratching and wondering about how your stock order ever got that big. No more surprises EVER.

Do ex hairdressers and beauty therapists make better reps?

I believe it makes no sense to have someone who isn't good at sales in the role of product company rep. Yet most of our company product reps are ex hairdressers or therapists. They seem to gravitate to the role after years of over-work on the salon floor. It seems the next logical step and they get to stay in an industry they love.

19

At the considerable risk of offending someone, I'm going to be honest here and say the best reps I've come across are NOT ex salon staff. They are sales people who've come from sales backgrounds in other sectors. Sure, there are some great reps who are ex industry. If you're lucky enough to have one, you've had a double win. Michelle, my best-ever rep, was a hairdresser first, so they are out there.

The challenge is that some of them fall into the same traps as salon owners do. They get caught up in the emotion of the salon and start bending the rules for product ordering and payments. Rather than buying in to the excuses, they'd be better spending their time teaching the salon owner better retailing practices.

One of the things Michelle did well, along with Carlo from Ozdare, another rep of mine, was showing me where I sat in the scheme of things. Michelle might say: *You are in the top 10 of my salons for consistent growth.* Or: You are number four for number of units sold per month. Carlo might show me how my retail statistics compared to other salons that had the same number of clients. You know how much I value figures, right? This reality check was perfect for me. It made me feel good about our efforts while making me aware we could do better. Without these sorts of insights, it's easy to be caught up in the belief that everyone is average.

Good people are everywhere. Your job is to work with the product rep you get given. With clearer communication, you should be able to work out a plan you're both happy with.

Don't be a D account. If you work together on getting your retail sales up to the top of his/her accounts list, you'd soon have your product rep's attention.

Think about your worst salon client, the one who's always late, complains about the price and wants extra attention. Do you want to be like her?

Remember: you're a client to your product rep. Act with integrity and be the best client you can be. Your rep will value you and really look after you and your salon.

When all else fails.

If you absolutely can't get the outcome you want with the rep you're allocated, you need to go above that person and take up your concerns with the state manager. It's no different in your salon. If you had a client not happy with one of your team members wouldn't you prefer the client came to you to explain their point of view? I certainly always treasured the opportunity to fix the situation rather than lose the client. It's all part of running a great salon and so much of it is down to good communication. In the salon, with your product rep and with everyone else you have dealings with: treat everyone like you'd like to be treated and you can't go far wrong.

Kick-arse kick-starter.

Craft a short script to use next time a product rep phones or drops in to your salon unannounced. Learn it, practise it and be ready to handle the situation politely and efficiently.

19

twenty

chapter

One for the product reps.

Salon owners, here's your chance. I'm giving you a leg-up by including a chapter specifically written FOR product reps. It's what I think product reps need to hear – how salon owners view the product rep relationship and how you can work together for great outcomes.

Why not lend your copy of this book to your product rep? Or, even better, buy them a copy and hand it over with this chapter bookmarked.

You'll be doing yourself, your team, your product rep and all of us in the industry a big favour by spreading the word that there's always a better way for any of us to do our jobs.

Product reps, this is for you …

20

Business is business.

The salon has salon clients and you, the rep, have the opposite: clients that are salons.

No matter what business you're in, there are three things you should never take your eye off. These are the metrics you need to grow:

- The numbers of clients you see.
- What they spend with you.
- How often they return.

We teach this to salon owners and we drill down on why these are the be all and end all of successful business. What you need to be doing, in any business, is growing all three of these areas.

It's no different for the product company rep.

I often see great product reps getting bogged down in thinking they have to "do the right thing" and continue to service the D grade salons on their client list. No, you don't! In fact, it's time we cut the NICE stuff and worked on a more, open transparent way forward.

You might think I'm out of line. Hear me out and I'll explain myself.

The way I see it, your "business" is no different to any other business that puts huge amounts of energy into trying to please the smaller accounts.

Let's take an unemotional look at what's going on.

20

Take stock of who you stock.

If you were to move five of your worst accounts and replace them with five new ones, wouldn't your work day look much better?

Look at your accounts. What if you could build a plan to be in a much better place this time next year, with a client list that made you feel positive about servicing your salons and clinics?

Where do you start? By looking at the salon accounts you have right now and grading them A, B, C and D.

A grade accounts might look like this (or you might create your own guidelines):

- they pay on time
- their order is always above $X
- they order consistently, same day, every two weeks
- they engage with your whole offering
- they attend your industry events
- they put their hands up for training
- they're the clients you ask for a testimonial to show when you get new enquiries
- they run a great business
- they love working with you
- you love working with them

If all your accounts were like this, life would be a joy!

20

B grade salon clients would tick off most of these points, maybe missing one or two.

C grade would miss a couple more.

D grade? Well they're the opposite of A:

- they don't pay
- they don't stock the whole range
- they play the victim card
- they want free things
- and all the other shitty things that come with below-the-line thinking

> " *If you want* **serious results,** *you must get* **serious** *about who you hang around with.* "

Here's the truth. You have salon clients from right across the grading spectrum. That means you have the potential to increase one type or another. Blind Freddy knows that the A and B graders are the ones you want. Guess what? A grade people hang around with like-minded A grade people.

What excites me most is that I see where you could be doing so much better. It's no different to what we teach at ZING: work

20

harder on yourself, become the company of choice and the A grade clients will come.

I'm working on training designed for product companies to get to the reality of best practice when it comes to working with salons, both hair and beauty. It will be the roadmap you've been waiting for. I've listened to salon owners' frustration for the last five years. I know how they think. I understand the reality check that product reps need to face up to.

My program isn't centred on KPIs (key performance indicators). It's around your critical drivers. What is it you need to do to hit your KPIs? The must-do things that drive your sales to get the results you want. The outcomes will:

- increase the number of salons you see
- increase what each spends with you
- increase how often they place an order

My program will answer the burning question: *What is it you need to do today that will increase these three key metrics tomorrow?* It will be different for different brands but there's a central truth that's common to all. That's where my training is focused.

It's 2017, people.

Same old, same old is just that – it's the SAME and it's OLD.

It's 2017 and it's time to think differently. Apart from the product you sell what value can you add to a business?

I think it's rather boring and stale to keep saying, "Hello, here is my brochure. I can see you're busy. I'll leave it on the desk. See you next month."

That's been done to death. I ask you: *What else have you got?*

Let me tell you about Josh.

Josh is a rep who you can't help but like. He's an old soul wrapped in a young chap's body and he has a way with people.

He told me about how he charmed a salon owner to stock his brand by using his Nonna's sauce. I know … it's mental. But it worked!

The first couple of times he visited the salon, he couldn't get past the gatekeeper (the receptionist). Next time he sees the owner and seizes the opportunity.

He says, "Hi, I'm Josh and if you have five minutes I'd like to show you my water-saving tap heads for you basin. I'll be quick."

The salon owner was very impressed and changed his taps over, there and then.

The chap was Italian and so is Josh. They soon got talking about Italian families and, of course, Italian food.

The next month when Josh came to town, he did as he promised and dropped in to the salon to check everything was fine. He found the owner again and said, "I've been thinking about you and I'd like to look after you for more than just the taps."

He then handed a gift (a homemade bottle of tomato sauce) to the salon owner and said, "From one Italian family to another.

20

I'd like you to try my Nonna's pasta sauce."

"I'm also going to leave you a full-size sample of every product we stock. If you like them, we can talk next month, once you've had a chance to test them out."

Off he went. Next month he walked in and the chap said, "Hey, what did you put in those bottles?" Josh is worried, and wondering if it's a trick question.

"Because the team absolutely love them, and you're right, you need to look after me."

That was how it started. The working relationship and mutual respect was formed over Nonna's sauce. Josh got clever and creative, found some common ground and a way to make a real connection. And the salon owner's sales are fabulous, just like Josh.

See, you can choose who you want to work with (and who you don't). You just have to think outside the box to make it happen.

Agree to disagree.

Where exactly is the point at which you agree to disagree with a salon client and withdraw your brand?

There must be a cut-off point. A line in the sand where you'll stop them from stocking your product.

20

It needs to be a fair calculation that takes into account the size of the salon team.

Maybe something like: *if their monthly order isn't $X, then you can let them go.*

I suggest you quantify it in units rather than dollars. *If a salon can't move X units to solve X of their clients' problems in a month, you need to walk away.*

Consider devising a fair formula that takes into account the size of the salon team.

Then what? I suggest you have a private, one-on-one chat with the salon owners in these under-performing salons, and say something along these lines:

"We're making some changes and we want you to be a part of them. We're no longer going to stock the salons that order fewer than X products per month (that's Y products a week) We're prepared to do our part and we have a training program we want your whole team to be involved in. Here's a list of our training dates. The number of units we require you to order per month is X. Last month your order was Y, so we are Z units away from where we need to be. The company is also putting up some great prizes and we're very excited. The results are for everyone. This is base camp with our new program and I think you and your team could really step up with some training. I'll be doing all I can to support you. If you were to be selling Y products a week, that would mean an extra $Z in your pocket. Are you in?"

20

Why the big brands can afford to be picky.

Many of the big product brands don't let just anyone stock their product. It's clever – it creates a different mindset, changes the relationship to a "both in or nothing" one. You both – the rep and the salon – have to agree you're the right match.

The company allocates each salon a minimum order spend per month. Salon owners are often frightened away. Which is a good thing – it's exactly what the minimum is meant to do: eliminate the time-waster salons that aren't up to the standard, thereby creating an elite group of salons stocking the brand. It sorts out the client relationship before it even begins.

> ## "Take stock of who you stock. "

We do the same at ZING. I won't work with a salon owner who hasn't read my first book *The Naked Salon*. Why? Because it helps me sort out the time-wasters. If you can't make time to get through this easy-to-read book based 100% on the challenges you want me to help you with, then you are either not focused or the timing isn't right.

I get some doozies who ask me for help and when I ask if they've read my book, they say, "I've had a flick through it, but I just don't have the time". Sometimes it's a simple, "I'm not a book reader".

20

Experience tells me they'll flick through the advice and then flick through the systems I set up for them, too. They're like everyone else in the world; they get given 24 hours a day. How you spend your 24 hours is the difference between success and failure.

I heard of a personal trainer who only took on men who wanted to radically change their bodies. His program claimed to make them all as good in the bedroom as they were in the boardroom. It was a 12-week body program. He asked one question: "What did you have for breakfast this morning?" Depending on the answer, he decided if they'd be a suitable candidate and if he should take them on or not. If they skipped breakfast, he knew they weren't right for his program.

He charged a hefty fee of 10,000 pounds and made them pay another 2,000 pounds upfront in case they failed and damaged his brand. They only got the 2,000 pounds deposit back if they stuck to the program and radically transformed their bodies. It changed his business overnight. He was now calling the shots, not the clients. He'd drawn a very clear line in the sand to define what was acceptable. Those who did get accepted as clients felt lucky and were very committed to the program.

Let's get serious.

20

What is it you need to do to get pickier about who you work with?

Have you made your expectations clear?

What do you want from the salon clients that stock your brand?

Do you want to see your company's products displayed in a certain way?

Is it time your salon clients invested in educating themselves so they get better retail results? Maybe you could set a minimum number of education hours required per month or quarter so you know they're getting educated properly.

Is it more about enforcing a minimum monthly order size?

You'll know the answers that are right for you, your company and your salon clients. What I know is that this wishy-washy way of dealing with salons that don't take your product seriously and tick along in the "near enough world" are not doing you any favours.

If you want serious results, you must get serious about who you hang around with.

It's about you, too.

You also need to take a long, hard look at yourself. There's no excuse for poor representation by the company when the salon owner is fully committed to your brand. I know some fabulous salons located in remote areas and they never see a rep from one month to the next. With all the communication channels we have at our disposal today, it's simply not good enough that these salons are not serviced well. Face Time, Skype, Zoom, Join Me – there are countless ways to conduct a meeting virtually. Add these communication platforms into your new kick-arse plan and you'll see your sales doubling in no time.

20

What are you waiting for?

Go out and find the new accounts you need. Work closely with your existing A, B and some of the C grade accounts, implement a workable education program and get those orders booming. You and your salon owners need to work together on two keys: the truth and the training. And, finally, educate your salon clients on the benefits of more frequent ordering, especially as their metrics grow.

Remember my star? Go back to Chapter 2 and take another look. You're there, too. You're part of the success story. And you know what's amazing about this success story?

Everyone wins.

Kick-arse Kick-starter.

Check your list of salon client visits for tomorrow (just one day's worth to start). Go down the list and grade each one - A, B, C or D. Keep your gradings in mind during your visits and make a mental note of what you observe. My bet is you'll notice some fascinating behaviour patterns that will help make the way forward even clearer for you.

20

chapter

twenty one

21

Getting a grip on stock control.

Being overstocked with retail products is never a clever idea. But I'd rather your salon was overstocked than understocked.

To me, being out of stock screams disorganised. I recently ran out of a foundation I love and if I'd known how difficult it was to get, I would have bought two. I wasn't aware how common "out of stock" has become in the hairdressing and beauty world.

I tried the first two or three salons that I knew stocked the brand of my foundation. Both gave me the same sad response: "I'm sorry, we're out of stock". Rather than go to the trouble of driving around to any more locations, I decided to use my phone. I had to ring three other salons that stocked that brand before I found someone with the product I wanted on their shelf.

You're probably thinking it must have been an uncommon brand. It wasn't – it was by Bodyography. It comes with an applicator stick and it's about the fourth one I've had. It's a perfect match to my skin and I just keep on buying it. During the process of trying to source my foundation, I was tempted to just find another product. Those of you who wear foundation know how scary it is to change brands. I loved this one.

You need to think about what happens when you get a reputation for not having stock.

When we lived in Gisborne the local hardware store was always out of the things you most wanted. How frustrating! It was a Mitre10 store and I nick-named it Mitre 2, because it only ever seemed to have two items out of ten.

> **“**
> *Find your*
> **goldilocks** *of retail,*
> *your **just right,**
> **not too little, not**
> **too much 99**

How do you solve your stock problem?

Order more frequently, with smaller orders you can manage. There's a big myth around ordering more frequently. Most of you order once a month. For me, that's too hard to manage – a big hurdle to leap over when you're compiling the order and when your delivery arrives. Break it down into more manageable chunks, say under $1,000 worth. It's a good place to start. If that's two weeks of retail sales for your salon, great.

It might only be one week's worth for some of you and, for others, just a couple of days. Weekly would be ideal – and a logical routine to work into your salon schedule.

What about those of you who are just learning to fly? I suggest you think about placing an order every two weeks and here's why.

You can keep a better grasp of things. If something's missing that didn't go through your order system, it will stand out. Someone stealing stock will also stand out. Sad, I know, but it happens.

With a sound and regular stock ordering plan in place, you won't ever overspend and you'll always know exactly what's going on. You should have your retail stock levels set to suit your salon demands and then just replace what you've sold.

Your back-end stock use is different and you'll likely need some help with figuring out a good system. There are some guidelines you can stick to once you've crunched a few numbers.

It's also worth setting up a direct debit every week to your product company for your average spend. You should be aiming to be an A grade client (see Chapter 18) so if you ever need a favour you can fall back on your great relationship with your product company. Paying your account on time and never falling behind is certainly A grade client behaviour.

Some salons are so influenced by freight charges, you'd think they're prepping for an outbreak of war. Not wanting to pay freight is petty and having thousands of dollars tied up on your shelves is pure madness.

21

I'll show you what I mean. Do this little sum for me and I bet you'll find you can reduce your retail stock by 80 products. All the product lines that you're carrying 3 or 4 units of (and selling almost none of), change those stock levels to 2 units. Now, look at the product lines you do sell often. If you sell 4 each week, then you need to have 20 at the start of the month. You can't put them all out on display, so you have other spots where you must store them, right? Far too hard in my opinion.

Only have what sits out the front on your display shelf. If you were to order every two weeks with say 80 fewer products, this is what you'd have.

Say a product is $18 at cost, so 80 of them costs you $1,440. That's money sitting about on your product shelf. Couldn't you better use those dollars to pay down a credit card or sit on your home loan in redraw? Either would be an improvement on sitting on your salon shelf fading in the sun.

If, instead of monthly, you ordered every two weeks, and paid $15-$25 in freight, you'd be placing 26 more orders a year at an additional cost of $390-$780. Some of you will be paying more in freight and some will have more than 80 products lolling around doing nothing other than sunbaking under your lighting waiting for their turn to go home with a client.

My point is: be stocked properly but make sure you're not overdoing it or underdoing it. Find your goldilocks of retail, your "just right, not too little, not too much".

Your stock presentation is critical.

I've seen some exceptional, whizz-bang stock merchandising. And I've seen the odd train wreck. For inspiration, think of the lovely AESOP stores – elegant and simple displays that are very consumer friendly. That's where you need to aim. If you haven't been inside an AESOP store, put it on your to-do list.

Your clients expect top-notch attention to detail when it comes to retail displays, especially for high-end products. I know I've been put off a purchase by the dust or fade on a product box. If it's sat there long enough to gather dust or fade, I get to wondering about why no one else wants this product. It's much less desirable to me. Something to watch if your product shelves get direct light.

Some high-end beauty products aren't even stored on the general shelf as the light can affect how well they work. That, and the fact they're often priced around $150 each so best kept where they can be counted! Perhaps you can keep just one of each on display? I've seen that work. Do whatever you need to do. Just do it well. Make sure every product is clearly marked with the correct price. There's nothing worse than a team member fumbling around in front of a client trying to work out what an item retails for.

A challenge just for hair salons.

This one doesn't relate to beauty – it's a challenge just for hair salon owners. I love when you stock great products and also commit to using them at the basin. If you don't, you're sending your clients mixed messages.

Some people, no matter how much money they have, would never buy a $45 shampoo and a $45 conditioner. I saw this first-hand. One year I gave my sister a shampoo and conditioner gift pack for her birthday without realising I'd left the price sticker on the bottom. When she screamed "Holy shit!" from the bathroom I ran in asking, "Are you OK?"

"This shampoo pack retails for $90!" she said. "Some people must have way too much money. I wish I'd known earlier. I would have sold it on EBay before I opened it." She's hilarious, but it made me think about where people place value and how we just take it for granted that we never have to pay full whack.

"Just use it and enjoy it," I told her. "You paid nothing. It was a gift, remember."

She did and she absolutely loved it. There's no way she would have purchased that product with her own money. She had no complaints with what she was already using and she'd never experienced the difference.

Sadly, most of our clients are just like my sister. You need to win their trust and then they'll listen to your advice. Nobody cares how much you know until they know how much you care. We, as professionals, know so much more than our clients about what products will bring them the most benefits, the products that will solve their problems. If you care about your clients, you will share the secrets that we just take for granted.

> " *Nobody cares how much you know until they know how much care.* "

Most people don't realise how concentrated a salon strength product is. I'm using a cleanser now that's so concentrated I use an amount half the size of a pea (and that's usually too much). People need education on more than one level.

Like many salon owners, you're probably pulling your hair out over your basin stock. How do you stop your team routinely pumping out two pumps at the basin, and wasting huge amounts of product? Understand that they don't know any better until you explain their zealous pumping frenzy is just making the product company richer. Tell them their loyalty is better placed closer to home, with you.

I've seen salon owners stretch rubber bands around the pump to stop a full pump, only to find team members pumping four times (every time). Instead, your team should care about you and go out of their way to not be wasteful. And "care" is the best way I know to solve this problem. Teach your team to care enough to show the client the correct amount of product to use. Doing that every time, not only shares knowledge and educates clients, it also reduces product waste.

Tell your team the facts: "Because you're all heavy-handed,

I must replace on average four of the one litre basin stock every three weeks. At $40 a litre, that's $160."

Go deeper and explain that over a year, you do that 17 times for a total spend of $2,720. "If you didn't double pump, I'd be likely to spend half of that instead, saving $1,360."

Imagine the results in your salon, if you put those savings towards education for your team.

Of course, your salon will be different. Simply substitute your own figures in the above conversation. If you take the time to explain the facts to your team members, you'll discover they do care and they'll be glad to change their behaviour to help you (and your clients) out.

Your other option is to use a more affordable shampoo at the basin. Some clients are never going to purchase a high-end product from you. If you have a conversation during your consultation about what they're already using, you'll know what option to take when you get to the basin.

I once met a salon owner who insisted his team always start with a deep cleanse shampoo. It was like a primer; everyone got it. It was one of those no-name brands sourced from a salon supplier. Maybe that's taking it too far, but if you can't get your team to respect the products you supply them with, it could be a valid option.

You need at least two price points when it comes to what you stock. It's better for your clients to get your recommendation at every price point. You and I know that your clients would be better off with the higher-end product but you must respect that it's their choice. Remember: the mark-up is the same at any price point. And you having their business is always better than Coles having it.

There's a café in Melbourne's famous Queen Victoria Market that only makes coffee using full-cream, homogenised milk. I was outraged when I asked for soy milk and was told "we don't do soy." It was as though they were happy to say they didn't do soy. Smug, even. I was reminded of that sketch in the English sitcom *Little Britain* where the "Computer says NO". The café always seems to be busy. I can't help imagining how much busier they'd be if they offered both skinny milk and soy milk, too.

I know – some people don't agree with me; they're sold on just the one range and the one price point, and that's all they stock. If their clients don't like it, it's too bad. For me, that means problem not solved, sale not made.

Bottom line is it's your salon: you can't be everything to everyone; you decide where to draw the line.

Kick-arse kick-starter.

Do you have any "double-pumpers" on your team? There's only one way to be sure – consciously keep an eye on your team at the basin for the next few days and see if you have a problem. Then you know what you're dealing with.

chapter

twenty two

Out of the blocks and beyond your blockages.

If you really want to change, you need to focus on three critical areas, or steps:

1. The intention to succeed.

2. A solid plan using the 10 x 10 x 10 strategy.

3. A look back at where you have failed before.

If you've made it this far, I'm going to assume you have the mindset you need to make change happen. If you want this bad enough, you'll make it a reality. I've seen so many people succeed, and it's a pleasure to watch every single one of them.

You're in charge of your day. If you're like me and want the best for your clients, you'll get a little uneasy. Embrace what's beyond your comfort zone and move step-by-step towards recommending retail products being just what you do. No different to putting a towel under a cutting wrap or asking someone to stand in a certain way so you can give them the best possible spray tan.

As I say to everyone I coach, mentor or present to: *I'm not asking you for a kidney, people. I'm just asking you to put your emotion aside and consider the client in front of you.*

You've got your head in the right space, so what's your plan? Is it to put every product you use in front of the client and simply say, "This is what I am using on your hair today because … or this is the sunscreen I think you should be using because …"

Is it your plan that everyone leaves your salon with a product or a sample?

This book is full of great ideas. Now, it's your turn. Begin with the idea that feels right for you and your salon, and put your own spin on it. You must own it – that means you have to adapt it to be your version.

Next, ask yourself where you're going to make a start and when. Set a date, talk to your team, work out what change you're happy to begin with and build your way up to add in every strategy.

It's no different to learning any skill. You start with something simple like a half leg wax. No one starts with a Brazilian – you work your way up to that, gradually building the skill and confidence to do the more complicated services. My tip is to be realistic. Set yourself and your team up to win and have some fun, so you feel good. Then you'll be happy stepping it up a notch.

Use the 10 x 10 x 10 as a guide.

Focus on the first 10 days (that's 2 weeks). You're not counting the days you don't work. If you're part-time, it will take you longer. It'll be hard going at times. If you're using my "every client, every time" rule, you'll need to put in a big effort not to slip up.

Here's the good news: the next 10 days will be the worst. Some days will feel unbearable but you can't let yourself slip back into autopilot. Focus on what you're doing. Expect it to take time to feel settled, as you would in a new job.

The following 10 days (days 11 to 20) are going to be 100 times easier. Sure, you'll feel uncomfortable at times but nothing like you did during the first 10 days.

22

Then guess what? Most people think change takes 21 days, that you need 21 days to form a new habit. I disagree. On day 21, you're out of the red zone but you can't yet lock it in as your new way of doing things. The next 10 days (days 21 to 30) are your critical "lock this shit down" stage. If you don't complete the full 10 x 10 x 10 program, your subconscious mind is still trying to tell you, "That was way too hard. I had to use my brain."

If you stick to it and complete the 10 days of "lock this shit down" you'll form a habit that will stick with you for good.

I experienced this first hand at yoga. I used to go 3 to 4 times a week. Even though I loved it, I hadn't thought about going more often. One day they put up a challenge at the yoga studio – to go to yoga every day for 30 days. I love a challenge, so I stepped up and went every day. Some days, I found it hard going to get there but I'd made up my mind. I hadn't even considered that in the process of stepping up to the challenge, I was forming a new habit simply by sticking to it for 30 days. The first 10 were unbearable, the next 10 were uncomfortable and the last 10 made me unstoppable.

Now, if I don't go every day, I feel I'm missing out. Going every day has become my normal. That's what I want for you when it comes to your retail sales – that you do the 30 days of bootcamp and never look back.

How cool would it be to have your clients' needs met all the time? How good would it feel to be your product company's favourite salon, to get invited to VIP events? How good would life be when you always have enough money to pay your salon bills and to pay yourself a fabulous wage? To be paid what you're worth? I'd be delighted to get every salon out of struggle street. I've never met a salon with healthy retail that didn't have a fantastic loyal client base. It starts and ends with your client care.

22

Where have you been going wrong?

Now, let's put a spotlight on where you've failed in the past. There are lessons to be learned in your past. I'll take you through the most common blockages people have around sales. Can you see yourself in some or all of them? Be honest with yourself, here. The truth is your only way forward.

Blockage #1: You're scared of the word NO. No one enjoys spending time and energy explaining to a client why they should invest in your idea only for them to say, "No, I'm not interested". We'd all much rather hear, "That's just what I need, thank you! I'm so pleased you told me that".

If you take the emotion out if it, you'll find it much easier.

You have to think differently about the word NO.

Imagine you're doing a client's makeup and you ask if she likes eyeshadow in grey tones. She says, "No, I only like natural earthy brown". Would that offend you? If you suggest a client goes a lot shorter with her hairstyle and she says, "NO, I like the length it is now" – would you be offended? I hope not.

It's just someone's opinion.

Retail is exactly the same. You think your client would be better off going ahead with your suggestion. Your client thinks she'd be better off not. That's it. Does that mean you stop making suggestions? NO. Sometimes your client takes your advice. Sometimes your client doesn't. It's not personal. It's just what it is.

> **" You have to think *differently* about the word NO. "**

You need to get over your fear of NO and put your energy into getting a YES. Then you get to put on that face I love – the one where you've asked your client if she'd like to take all three products you used on her today and, to your shock, she says YES. You rush out the back to share your news with the team: *OMG! She is taking all three!* Then you rush back out, get a bag and take her money before she changes her mind. We all do it! It's all part of the reward of a job well done.

Blockage #2: You're letting your glass ceiling show. Without even knowing it, most of us have a glass ceiling when it comes to money. Do you falter when you have to ask for a certain dollar figure from a client? For example, "That's $236. Are you paying by card?" Right there. That's your glass ceiling. It's clear and you can't actually see it but it's there. When the account gets over $300 you panic a little. You look at the computer to see where you can pull it back under $300, maybe just to $299. Sound familiar? Your glass ceiling might be at $350. Or $400. If you're really lucky, you don't have one. But most of us do, so be honest with yourself.

What I know for sure is this: if your client is running up a bill that high, they must have spent the best part of a day with you. You might want to think about charging them rent as well. LOL.

No one should ever be shocked when the account is high. If you've done your job and at the beginning asked if your client wants a price quote, you've covered yourself.

Sometimes you've got your face so squished up against your glass ceiling, you decide to knock the final figure down to something more palatable, only to have your client say, "Is that all? I thought it was going to be heaps more." Clear proof that the glass ceiling I'm talking about is all in your head.

The price you charge your client is what it is. Any retail component in the price is a necessary part of caring for your client between visits. If anything, it's a measure of your care factor. Think about that and charge fairly and correctly. Every client, every time.

Blockage #3. You judge people. Everyone judges others and, in general, there's not a problem with that. Unless by judging them, you're cutting them short, making decisions for them. We all look at the way people are dressed and maybe admire. We're judging that they have good taste. And we look at others who aren't to our liking and judge them in a way that's biased or unfair.

We've all been guilty of this when it comes to recommending retail, haven't we? It comes back to treating everyone equally. Your client has made their way to your salon of their own free will, chosen your business because they're expecting a certain level of care. For you not to deliver on their expectations doesn't make sense. It's easy to judge older people as not having money because grey hair and wrinkles can often mean they're no longer earning an income. If you're making assumptions like that, you could be very wrong.

My cool client Marg was in her late seventies. I remember her telling me that one of the things she particularly liked about our salon was that we didn't treat her like a senior. What a lovely compliment. Don't assume you have to offer a senior discount. We didn't have a senior price and no one ever seemed to notice or question it.

In my salon, we gave everyone a full service and charged them a full price. But I learned it the hard way. I once lent an $85 hairpiece to a young girl for her debutante ball. I assumed that, at her age, she wouldn't have money for the hair-up *and* the hairpiece. Until she showed me the sparkly pins she'd bought to put in her hair. The pins came with a $115 price tag. Turns out my $85 hairpiece was very affordable.

Everyone finds the money for the things they see value in. Spend your time showing your clients the value – some will see it, some won't. Their choice, not yours.

Blockage #4 You forget. Often "I forgot" is nothing more than a bullshit excuse (see Chapter 5). But sometimes you genuinely forget. The kicker is this: if you don't have a system in place, you are always going to be pushed to remember to recommend retail. Create a system that builds retail into your every time, every day client care and you'll never forget.

I'm a visual person so I need to see my cues. I always started with the shampoo and conditioner. I placed them on the bench in front of my client and simply said, "This is what I used on you today." That was it. Then, every product I used in their hair, I explained what I used and why. I showed them how much to use and where to place it in their hair. For every product, I grabbed an unopened one from the product shelf and put it in front of them. It took some time for me to lock it down as my every client, every time routine. To this day, when I'm shampooing my 89 year-old mum's hair over the kitchen sink, I look at the shampoo bottle and I say, "This is what I'm using on you today, because …" I do the same for Muriel my dog when I'm washing her. "Muriel, I'm using flea shampoo on you because…" Best I don't mix those two bottles up, hey?

It's now in my DNA. Now it is what it is. There's no chatter in my head telling me not to forget. It's a very good place to be.

Now I can just get on with the creative side, the fun side – the side I joined this mad industry for in the first place.

22

Kick-arse kick-starter.

Decide where you'll start. What is the one idea (of the dozens I've shared in this book) that resonates with you? Begin with the idea that feels right for you and your salon ... and get out of the blocks.

twenty three

chapter

23

Retail care explained.

By now, you're convinced and committed to this journey of making your salon retail rock, right?

From here, it's all about gathering the tools you need, bedding in the practices and making recommending retail second nature for you and your team.

This chapter pulls together the big principles, ideas and tips in a nifty wordplay to help you and your team recall what's important.

At the end, I'll tell you how to download a version to keep handy as an all day, every day reminder.

R.E.T.A.I.L. C.A.R.E. explained.

R. Build **RAPPORT.** People only buy from people they know, like and trust. If you haven't used your smarts to let the client know you're an expert in your field, you've missed an opportunity to help someone.

E. Clients today are looking for two things: an experience and an **EXPERT.** Gone are the days when people just took your word for things. Want to stand out? Know your products and the benefits they deliver.

T. Stop selling to people. Instead, **TELL** them what you know. Share your knowledge freely. If you're generous with your knowledge the sale will come. Just tell people what you know – they'll be grateful.

A. Asking clients about their biggest hair problem will open up a conversation about how you can solve it for them. You must **ASK** or you won't know. Don't assume things. Get in there and ask. People appreciate that you want to solve problems for them. Don't be shy. Listen for clues.

I. If clients are hesitant to buy, **INVITE** them to sample products first. Everyone should leave your salon with a product or a sample of a product. Not sometimes. Every time.

L. LEARN everything there is to know about the products you stock. You'll be amazed at how much your confidence grows. People are drawn to confidence. Don't underestimate the value of working on your confidence.

C. Client **CARE** includes making retail recommendations, often and freely. If you're not considering what your clients are using at home between visits, you're only doing half your job. If you **CARE** about your clients, you'll share your knowledge. The uncomfortable sales "chatter" in your head is just that – chatter. Once you accept it's OK if someone doesn't take your recommendations, you'll be free to get on with the job of caring for your clients.

A. ACTION it now. Right now. If you use or mention any product, stop right there and go grab it from the product shelf. It makes sense to both show and tell. You need to develop your own system. You know how annoying it is when you leave a store without what you came for? It's the same in your business. The issue is you're often under the pump and your good intention about keeping up kills the retail sale. It takes seconds to stop, grab the product and keep on running … like Forest Gump.

R. REALITY check. It's not your money. Don't judge where people should or shouldn't spend their money. I'd hate for someone to decide for me where I should spend my money. I'm guessing you're the same. Don't judge if people have the money to spend. Just get on with recommending.

E. EVERYONE is entitled to professional advice. Everyone. Always use the product name when you ask if they'd like to take it home with them today. Don't miss the important part – closing the sale – just because you feel uncomfortable at the prospect of getting a NO. Everyone gets a big fat NO some of the time. That's OK. It's not about you getting a NO and getting all emotional. It's about you just doing your job. Instead, celebrate the people you helped who said YES.

Kick-arse kick-starter.

Go to www.zingretailresources.com.au and download our handy poster version of Retail Care Explained. Stick it on your fridge, noticeboard, toilet door or wherever you and your team can see it all day, every day.

23

chapter

twenty four

24

The 70/30 rule.

Have you ever thought about how the yackety-yak-yak you do every day affects your salon success, especially your retail performance?

24

I'll be blunt. You need to shut up, talk less and listen more. We're made with two ears and one mouth for very good reason.

Consider the number of topics you cover that have nothing to do with hair, beauty or the reason your client came to see you today. You know, the fluffy stuff: *what my boyfriend said to me this morning, how I'm going to cook the turkey for Christmas this year, who I ran into at the local pub last week, blah, blah, blah.*

ALL the time, when I'm in and out of salons, I hear hairdressers and beauticians yackety-yak-yakking on about everything except the client's needs. It's as though you feel the need to entertain your clients. Trust me, you are not there to amuse. That's not what they pay you for. And there's no way you'll achieve the level of success you want (and I want for you) unless you stop yacking mindlessly and put your focus towards sticking to your plan.

I was told a long, long time ago about the 70/30 rule. It was exactly what I needed to hear at the time and it's stuck with me because it smacks of truth. And because it works.

The 70/30 rule goes like this: 70% of the conversation belongs to the client – it's up to them to choose the topic/s. If they choose to have total silence, that's their right. The other 30% is yours, but not for senseless chit-chat. You need to spend *your* 30% doing your job of consulting before you begin, explaining the service as you go, recommending retail and suggesting when your client should return for their next visit. Yes, you need to fit all this into your 30%, without taking shortcuts or missing opportunities to educate and share your secrets. As you can see, if you're doing it right, there's zero time left for yackety-yak-yak.

I remember a joke that went like this:

A hairdresser asks the client, "How would you like your hair cut today?"

The client replies, "In complete silence."

Not only do we talk a lot, we miss talking about what really matters.

The 70/30 rule is a simple, easy-to-recall blueprint for making the most of your time with your client. Think about it. In any hour you have only 18 minutes in which to get through all the things you need to say. There's nothing like a time restriction to get you to focus your efforts on the important stuff. To stop filling the empty space with words. To stop talking for the sake of talking.

Pauses and fewer words are much more powerful. When it comes to making an impression or highlighting a message, less is more.

People who say less have an air of confidence about them.

Let me show you what I mean. How does this sound to you?

"I think you need to try this shampoo because I've had a lot of people tell me they've had some great results with it. It's good for your hair type and if you start using it you'll see the results you're looking for. It's great with frizz and that has always been a problem for you. It's concentrated, so it will last a long time. It's good value. You'll love it."

Or how about this?

"You soooo need this shampoo, it's unreal ..." Pause, wait for a response. Then you talk about the benefits.

Can you see that too much simply doesn't work? It's overwhelming. You're on to the next thought or message before your client's had time to absorb the first.

Staying on track.

Sometimes, your client drags you off the professional track, even when you set out with the best intentions. There are tricks for turning the conversation to where you want it to go.

Consider this scenario:

Your client shows up full of wonder about your time away and your recent trip to Bali. She comes through to the chair and even before she's seated, she's asking, "How was your trip? Did it rain much? Did you get to the café I suggested?"

What if you responded like this. "Yes, yes and sort of yes. First let's get onto the most important thing I have on today – your hair. Once I'm clear on the plan and what we're looking to achieve today, I'll gladly tell you all about my trip. In short, it was a fabulous holiday."

24

Now, you're in control of the conversation.

Don't ever forget the reason your clients come to you is to solve their problems. When you go off track, talking about all sorts of unrelated stuff, you're likely to miss the important stuff around caring for your client and recommending products.

So, how do you deal with the clients who show up so they can bitch and moan about their kids or their husband? Or always have a sad story about someone who's sick and insist on telling you *all* about them?

> **"People who say less have an air of confidence about them. "**

Try taking this tack.

You say: "How are you today?"

She says: "Not so good. My friend is so sick. We think she may have cancer and we're just waiting on word to find out if she has."

You say: "Dear me! You poor thing. I can't imagine how awful that must be. Can I suggest something? Let's make this time about you. Let's not talk about anything that will add to your sadness. I'd like to make this your best visit with me yet and that will be difficult if we talk about the sadness of your friend. Is that OK if we do that? First up, I want to talk about your hair and our plan for today…"

24

Once again, you're in control of the conversation.

Steering the conversation is an art you can practice. It's not hard once you get the hang of it. Of course, there are some of you who love the drama conversation so you end up listening when you shouldn't. Don't do that, it will wear you down and cost you your happiness in the end. I've seen people walk away from our industry because they've heard one too many divorce stories.

Your job is to do the service your client came for, not to listen to their life's drama. Is it possible to stop that chatter completely? Probably not. But I figure most of you could halve the amount of yackety-yak-yak you do and still not be within the desired 70/30 ratio!

Over to you.

The choice is yours. I wrote this book with your success in mind. It's time for you take action, to step up and make it happen.

Your success as a salon owner is in your hands. It's not rocket science, it's about hard work and doing it smarter. Your success is based on being the expert your client expects and needs; you looking after your client while they enjoy an awesome experience. To be truly successful long-term, you'll need to be seeing half your clients taking a retail product home with them every time, week in, week out.

Without a doubt, your retail shelf is a measure of your business. A high turnover shelf where the products sell too fast to gather dust is a sure sign of a consistent and solid salon business that has a loyal following.

I know for certain, if you don't make the TIME to develop a TEAM who have the skill of recommending retail to your clients, you will always struggle.

The MONEY is hiding in your retail shelf.

Go and find it.

Other books in the series

This title is the third book in Lisa Conway's series focused on helping salon owners take their salon from Good to Great:

The Naked Salon: An essential guide to time, team and money for salon owners

Your Salon Team: The salon owner's guide to finding, motivating and keeping great staff

Your Salon Retail: The no-nonsense, no-hype guide to kick-arse retail in your salon business

You can purchase all three books online at **www.zingcoach.com.au**

About the ZING Project.

Lisa Conway created the ZING Project to close the gap between what salon owners deliver and what salon clients want.

The ZING project is where it all happens: speaking, coaching, mentoring, online/offline, book resources, videos and more.

Our mission is to give every salon owner the opportunity to learn and grow - so that demand for what your salon offers has clients queuing out your door and up the hill.

At ZING, we teach salon owners what you're expected to know but were never taught.

Find out all about the **ZING Project, ZING Coaching** and **Club ZING** at **www.zingcoach.com.au** or call ZING office on **+61 457 607 888** to book your private one-to-one conversation with a ZING Coach.